Believable

Believable

How the Old Testament Reveals
the Truth of the Resurrection

WADE MILAM

RESOURCE *Publications* · Eugene, Oregon

BELIEVABLE
How the Old Testament Reveals the Truth of the Resurrection

Copyright © 2024 Wade Milam. All rights reserved. Except for brief quotations in critical publications or reviews, no part of this book may be reproduced in any manner without prior written permission from the publisher. Write: Permissions, Wipf and Stock Publishers, 199 W. 8th Ave., Suite 3, Eugene, OR 97401.

Resource Publications
An Imprint of Wipf and Stock Publishers
199 W. 8th Ave., Suite 3
Eugene, OR 97401

www.wipfandstock.com

PAPERBACK ISBN: 979-8-3852-0670-4
HARDCOVER ISBN: 979-8-3852-0671-1
EBOOK ISBN: 979-8-3852-0672-8

03/13/24

All Scripture quotations, unless otherwise indicated, are taken from the Holy Bible, New International Version®, NIV®. Copyright ©1973, 1978, 1984, 2011 by Biblica, Inc.™ Used by permission of Zondervan. All rights reserved worldwide. www.zondervan.comThe "NIV" and "New International Version" are trademarks registered in the United States Patent and Trademark Office by Biblica, Inc.™

For my wife Courtney, the true love of my life
And for Drew, Cooper, Reese, and Emme

Contents

Preface

Marley was dead: to begin with. There is no doubt whatever about that. . . . There is no doubt that Marley was dead. This must be distinctly understood, or nothing wonderful can come of the story I am going to relate.

—*A CHRISTMAS CAROL,* CHARLES DICKENS

ALMOST EVERYONE HAS HEARD the tale of Ebenezer Scrooge and how the miserable, selfish miser was changed into a new man after a visit from the ghost of Jacob Marley. Marley's ghost showed Ebenezer the heavy chain that he carried through the afterlife because of his self-centered deeds, and warned that Ebenezer was headed for the same fate. It goes without saying that if Marley hadn't died there would be no ghost and, therefore, no story of redemption.

Surely almost everyone has also heard the fantastic tale of Jesus's life, death, and supposed resurrection. The intent of this book is to argue that such an unlikely tale is possible. However, it also depends on the acceptance of an underlying truth: no one at the time of Jesus's death was expecting a resurrection. The idea seemed as absurd to people living back then as it seems to many of us now. When the apostles began to preach that Jesus was risen from the dead, nobody said, "Oh yeah, just like it says in Leviticus 4." In fact, when Paul told the Roman governor Festus about the resurrection, Festus replied, "You are out of your mind, Paul! . . . Your great learning is driving you insane" (Acts 26:24).

The Jewish people were looking for God to send them a messiah, an anointed savior who would be equal parts warrior, priest, and king, to save them from foreign rule. However, they all regarded God as holy—so pure and good that no one could stand in his presence. The idea that God would inhabit the world as a man and die a shameful criminal's death was unfathomable to them.

Understanding that, it follows that when the apostles proclaimed Jesus as raised from the dead, they were either honestly relating what they had seen or retelling a desperate lie that they made up on the spur of the moment to try and save what was left of their movement. With that in mind, I believe it is possible that a study of several stories preserved in the Old Testament can, like Marley's ghost, allow something "wonderful [to] come of the story."

Abbreviations

ESV-English Standard Version

CT-Contemporary Torah

Introduction

THESE ARE THE FACTS that everyone agrees on: A little more than two thousand years ago, a boy was born to a poor family in a small town in Palestine. Not much is known about the first three decades of his life, but when he was around thirty years old he began to travel around the countryside teaching as a rabbi (religious instructor). He taught with an authority and knowledge of Old Testament Scripture that was unusual for an unschooled country bumpkin, and there were rumors that he performed miracles. He attracted a large following and this, coupled with his withering criticism of the religious power structure that was in charge of Jewish society at the time, brought him into conflict with the priests, elders, and scribes running the country. After three years of teaching, things came to a head during the Passover festival, a time where large numbers of Jews from all over the world came to Jerusalem. Palestine was occupied by the Roman Empire at the time, and the Jewish leaders convinced the Roman governor that this teacher was a threat to the stability of the region, possibly even fomenting a rebellion. The Roman governor, Pontius Pilate, had the man flogged and executed publicly via crucifixion.

That should have been the end of the story, as it was for countless rebels who came before and found an ignoble end at the hands of the Romans. However, in this case something unusual happened: the man's followers began to make outrageous claims that he hadn't been simply a man but was in fact the Son of God, and that he had been resurrected. Despite ferocious persecution, the movement grew and spread. It grew so much that after three hundred years a Roman emperor, Constantine, declared it to be the official religion of the Roman Empire. Today, more than two billion people worldwide profess to believe that this man, Jesus, was in fact the Son of God and was resurrected after his crucifixion.

How can so many people believe such an unlikely story? Is there any way that people living today, two thousand years or so after these events, can gain any valid insight into the truth of this story? Without any video footage of the miracles, without any post-resurrection pictures of Jesus walking around, it would seem that there is no chance of knowing whether these bizarre claims are real.

Clearly, the truth of this story depends on the presence of a spiritual component of our existence. In a purely materialistic universe, no one is going to be coming back to life after being dead for three days. A resurrection calls for a spiritual entity that exists outside of the laws of physics as we know them. Unfortunately, an invisible, immaterial deity is by nature difficult to detect. So, how can you know if a god exists? If there is a God, which if any of the many religions that try to describe this being are correct?

The Bible claims to hold these answers, but the only way to know if it contains actual truth or not is to read it. For many people, the idea of reading the Bible is about as appealing as working on their taxes. To be fair, the Bible is a very long book, with sometimes confusing and archaic language, as well as stories that seem like myths or fairy tales to a lot of modern readers. Why in the world would anyone want to spend valuable time on a book like that?

In his teachings Jesus quoted extensively from the Old Testament, a conglomeration of religious writings sacred to his contemporary countrymen, known by both them and Jesus as "the Law and the prophets." Understanding the way that those ancient writings relate to the story of Jesus reveals that they were inspired by a force operating outside of time.

I believe there are stories in the Old Testament that, in their content, have the key to both determining the truth of Jesus's claims and to further understanding his teachings. There are five stories in particular that I believe can accomplish this. The goal of this book is to walk through the Old Testament using these five narratives as a guide—and by studying their undeniable, intrinsic connections to Jesus, prove that the Bible is a book inspired by a God who exists outside of time. These stories were written to prove that the death and resurrection of Jesus had been planned centuries before it came to pass. I invite you to take a look at these five accounts, and see if you agree.

Chapter 1

Joseph–The Only Beloved Son
Genesis 12, 15 and 25–50

To UNDERSTAND HOW THE BIBLE contains proof that Jesus was who he claimed to be, there are two important things that you must understand. First, you need a basic understanding of the structure of the Bible. It is divided into two main parts, the Old Testament and the New Testament. The Old Testament details the history of the Hebrew nation, beginning with the creation of the world and ending somewhere around the year 400 BC. The New Testament follows the life of Jesus and the establishment of the church after his death and resurrection.

The second critical point to understand is that the Bible, specifically the Old Testament, is old. Really, really old. Even compared to the New Testament, the Old Testament is ancient. The first book, Genesis, was believed for centuries to be the work of Moses, which would make it nearly 3,500 years old. Think about that for a minute. Twenty years ago there was no internet. One hundred and thirty years ago there were no cars or electricity. Five hundred years ago there were almost no Europeans living on the North American continent. One thousand years ago Europe and Asia Minor were ruled by the Holy Roman and Byzantine empires, respectively, and the many separate clans of Great Britain had only recently joined to form a unified kingdom. Two thousand years ago, all those areas were ruled by the Roman Empire in its prime. It is hard to fathom the amount of time that the book of Genesis has been a part of the human experience. To be fair, some modern scholars believe that Genesis was compiled and redacted by different authors with different agendas over a long period of time, but even the most recent estimates acknowledge that Genesis has existed in its present iteration since at least the fifth or sixth century BCE. That date is important because it means that Genesis predates Jesus by *at least* five hundred years.

Okay, so the Bible is divided into two parts, both old but one much older than the other. Why should anyone care how old the relative parts of the Bible are? Reading and understanding the stories presented in the Old Testament show that they predict the events of the New Testament hundreds of years before they actually occurred. And not just in a vague, "There will be this guy with brown hair" kind of way; I mean amazingly specific predictions that are impossible to explain without the existence of a timeless entity overseeing them. If you are skeptical, I don't blame you. Taken at face value, it seems pretty unbelievable. If you are open-minded enough to look at just one example, though, I think you will find some truth to it. The example I am referring to is found in Genesis, the first book of the Old Testament.

Genesis covers a lot of material. It is a book of history, which begins with an account of the creation of the universe, the earth, and the human race. It tells the story of humankind in general before narrowing its focus to Abraham, the father of the Israelite nation, and his descendants. Abraham is critical to this story, even though he is not the main character in it. In Genesis we find Abraham, just a regular guy, hanging out in a city called Haran. Out of nowhere, God told him to leave his city and his extended family to move to an unknown land. Abraham obeyed, even though there is no indication that he'd had any significant interaction with God prior to that time.

To reward him for his obedience, God made Abraham a promise consisting of three parts. The first two parts of the promise are found in Genesis 12:2–3: "I will make you into a great nation and I will bless you . . . and all people on earth will be blessed through you." The third part of the promise comes later, in Genesis 15:5: "Look up at the heavens and count the stars—if indeed you can count them . . . so shall your offspring be."

If you plucked anyone randomly from the pages of human history, it is pretty unlikely that they or their descendants would qualify as fulfilling any of those three criteria. And yet for Abraham, if you accept him as the father of the Hebrew people, undoubtedly two of these promises had come true. First, he was definitely made into a great nation. His descendants David and Solomon ruled as sequential kings of the most powerful kingdom in their part of the world at the time. Secondly, it is indisputable that Abraham's offspring are innumerable, as tens or even hundreds of millions of Jewish people have lived and died since that promise was made.

It is the third part of the promise, that "all people on earth will be blessed through you" that is much harder to evaluate. What in the world would count as something that blessed *everybody* in the world? Being the father of modern medicine? Discovering and harnessing electricity? Inventing the shot clock?

It would take something much better than any of those to qualify as fulfilling that particular promise. Much of later Jewish society expected it to come true in the form of the Messiah, who they expected to be a warrior/priest/king who would conquer all nations and set up a dynasty that would last for all time. God had a different plan, and beginning in the later parts of Genesis it is laid out in detail, thousands of years before it actually came to pass.

So our story starts in the second half of the book, which is concerned almost exclusively with the patriarchs of Israel and their wives. Abraham and his wife Sarah had a son named Isaac. Isaac married Rebekah and they had two sons, Jacob and Esau. Jacob married Rachel and had many sons, one of whom is the focus of our study. The blueprint for God's plan to bless the entire world is hidden in the story of Joseph, a son of Jacob, the last patriarch.

The story of Joseph takes up the last thirteen chapters of Genesis. To understand it, you need to know a little bit about his father Jacob. The story of Jacob is somewhat long but important; you can read it for yourself in Genesis 25–35. Jacob was not the most ethical individual ever. He was the younger of two twins, and his brother Esau stood to inherit most of the family's possessions as his birthright. Through a complicated process outlined in Genesis 27–28, Jacob tricked his father into giving him the birthright and the blessing that went with it. Jacob's brother Esau was naturally pretty upset, and his temper was such that Jacob ran away rather than face him. After wandering for a while Jacob came to his uncle's house, where he promptly fell in love with his cousin Rachel, which was OK back then. He agreed to work for his uncle for seven years in exchange for Rachel's hand in marriage, which seems like a pretty long time. However, Genesis 29:20 says that his feelings for Rachel were such that the time "seemed like only a few days to him because of his love for her." Unfortunately for Jacob, his uncle Laban was also a morally ambiguous individual; on the wedding night he switched out his older daughter, Leah, for Rachel. Maybe she had on a burka, or it was really dark, or Jacob was drunk, but for whatever reason he did not realize until morning that he had married the wrong woman. Understandably upset, he confronted his uncle, who told him he would have to work seven *more* years if he wanted to marry Rachel. With no other recourse, Jacob agreed to another seven years, which likely did not seem like only a few days to him this time around.

But finally, at last, Jacob had what he wanted. Sort of. He was married to two sisters, who were both his cousins. What could go wrong? Somewhat predictably, Leah and Rachel did not get along. Unfortunately for women who lived in that time period, much of their societal worth was tied to their ability to have children. Leah was a baby-making machine. She quickly had four sons, named Reuben, Simeon, Levi, and Judah. Rachel did not have any children, which left her feeling inferior and undervalued. Genesis 30:1 tells us that she was so upset that she told Jacob, "Give me children, or I'll die!"

At this point in the story I begin to feel a little sorry for Jacob. I mean, it sounds like he wasn't always the nicest guy, but he spent years working as an indentured servant to marry the woman he loved and now she was demanding that he give her children. What was he supposed to do? I feel nervous when my wife asks me to fix the sink. And anyway, Jacob was clearly not the problem, since Leah was making babies as fast as she could. Rachel's solution was to let Jacob start sleeping with her maidservant, whose children would count as her own. Jacob acquiesced and soon Rachel's servant Bilhah was having babies. Of course that did not sit well with Leah, who was in danger of falling behind; she demanded that Jacob sleep with *her* servant Zilpah, so that she could have babies for Leah. It was like some strange, dysfunctional multiverse version of *The Brady Bunch*.

Almost unbelievably, things got even weirder around his house. At one point we are told that Reuben, Leah's oldest son, had gathered some mandrakes for his mother. Apparently at that time mandrakes were thought to have some kind of efficacy as an aphrodisiac and/or fertility drug. Perhaps Leah, still trying to make Jacob love her, was hoping to use them in an effort to be more attractive to him. Rachel had her own ideas for the mandrakes, possibly wanting them as a fertility aid. She politely asked if Leah would share any of them with her; Leah refused, saying "Wasn't it enough that you took away my husband? Will you take my son's mandrakes too?" (Gen. 30:15). Ignoring her sister's creative revisionist history, Rachel offered to let Leah sleep with Jacob for the night if she would give up the mandrakes. Leah readily agreed, and in Genesis 30:16 we are told, "when Jacob came in from the fields that evening, Leah went out to meet him. 'You must sleep with me. . . . I have hired you with my son's mandrakes.'" Again, I have some sympathy for Jacob here. Doubtless many (boorish, uncultured) men might think that having four wives would be like living in some kind of fantasy. Jacob, however, had gone from dreaming of being married to a woman he loved so much that he was willing to work *seven years* to get her to being used as a sexual pawn in a power struggle between two unhappy sisters and their servants. On this day Jacob trudged home from a hard day in the fields, maybe just wanting to crack open a beer and sit in his recliner. Instead, he found Leah, so eager that she went out to meet him instead of waiting for him to get home, telling him that she had essentially rented him for the night. Not exactly the makings for a Hallmark movie.

At some point Jacob, likely exhausted, stopped having children. At that time he did not have any actual sons or daughters with Rachel, the true love of his life. The Bible tells us, though, that "Some time later . . . God remembered Rachel" (Gen. 30:21–22), and she gave birth to a son, Joseph.

This is the point of our whole long, convoluted story: while Jacob had many sons by four different women, Joseph, his youngest son, was the only child he had with Rachel (at that time). As a result we are told that Jacob, now called Israel, "loved Joseph more than any of his other sons, because he had been born to him in his old age; and he made an ornate robe for him" (Gen. 37:3).

THE STORY OF JOSEPH

This is where the story of Joseph begins. I know it took a while to get here, but it was important to understand the context. Jacob, who didn't get along with his brother Esau and lived his entire married life with two feuding sisters, started his own family down the same path. I mean, it's one thing to kind of have a favorite son, but when you announce that your youngest son is your favorite by giving him an ornate robe, it seems like you are asking for trouble. It may not seem like a big deal to us now, but giving Joseph an ornate robe back then was like buying him a new BMW while his brothers were all driving old beat-up pickup trucks. It is hard to imagine that such a gift would not cause hard feelings.

There may have been a way for Joseph, realizing that his privileged position caused his brothers to resent him, to try and make an effort to reach out and assuage their feelings of anger and injustice. Unfortunately, Joseph either didn't get it or just didn't care. In Genesis 37, we are told that Joseph had a dream where his brothers, symbolized by sheaves of wheat, all bowed down to him. Joseph, either arrogantly callous to or naively unaware of his brothers' hatred towards him, casually mentioned to them that he had a dream in which they were all his servants. The text also tells us, somewhat unsurprisingly, that they hated him even more for his talk about his dreams. Joseph was undeterred. He had a second dream where the sun, moon, and eleven stars were bowing down to him. In a family with a father, mother, and eleven brothers it didn't take a Nostradamus to interpret the meaning. True to form, Joseph told his whole family about this dream also. Family meetings on *The Brady Bunch* always seemed to make things better, but this one did not go so well. Even Jacob, Joseph's father and biggest fan, was a little taken aback by the apparent lack of humility, saying "What is this dream you have dreamed? Are we to come, I and your mother and your brothers, and bow low to you to the ground?" (v. 10 CT). By this point Joseph's brothers "were wrought up with him" (v. 11 CT) and "hated him so that they could not speak a friendly word to him." (v. 4 CT).

So there Jacob was, with a large contentious family. He had ten older sons who passionately hated his youngest son, in large part because of Jacob's overt favoritism. How would a thoughtful, caring father handle a situation like that? How would he diffuse the tension and bring his family together so they could find peace and healing? Unfortunately for his family, Jacob lacked either the will or the capability to hide his favoritism and unite his children. As the story progressed, the ten older brothers had taken the family's livestock to find better pastures. Joseph had been kept home, which likely didn't seem fair to the others. Then Jacob decided to send his youngest son, alone, to check up on his brothers. What could possibly go wrong?

When Joseph's brothers saw him coming, they were not very happy to see him. Their hatred of him had grown to the point that they decided to kill him. "Here comes that dreamer! . . . Come now, let's kill him and throw him into one of these cisterns and say that a ferocious animal has devoured him. Then we'll see what becomes of his dreams" (vv. 18–20). Thankfully for Joseph, his oldest brother, Reuben, had more of a conscience than the others and convinced them to just throw him in the cistern alive. Reuben's plan was to come back and rescue him later, but before he could a trading caravan passed by and the other brothers sold Joseph to the traders as a slave. They probably got some pleasure in the irony of seeing the boy who had predicted he would rule them all being carried away in chains to begin a lifetime of slavery.

To cover their tracks, the brothers took Joseph's fancy coat, dipped it into the blood of a goat, and took it back to their father Jacob. "We found this," they said. "Examine it and see whether it is your son's robe" (v. 32). Jacob, recognizing the garment as Joseph's, assumed that he had been killed by a wild animal. Devastated with grief, Jacob refused to be comforted.

Meanwhile, Joseph was taken to Egypt and sold as a slave into the household of Potiphar, the captain of the guard for the pharaoh. We are told that God was with Joseph in such a way that whatever he did prospered. Potiphar recognized Joseph's success and eventually placed him in charge of his entire household. Joseph was so efficient that Potiphar "left everything he had in Joseph's care; with Joseph in charge, he did not concern himself with anything except the food he ate" (Gen. 39:6). Unfortunately, Potiphar was not the only one who appreciated him; Potiphar's wife took notice of Joseph, who we are told was well built and handsome. She attempted to seduce Joseph, but he refused to betray his master's trust or to sin against God. Frustrated, she grabbed his cloak one day and attempted to pull him into her bed; Joseph fled, leaving her clutching his garment. When Potiphar returned home that day, he found his wife with Joseph's cloak, claiming that Joseph had attempted to rape her. Burning with anger, Potiphar threw Joseph into prison.

At this point it seems to be a riches-to-rags story, with the hero going from the favored son in a prosperous family to a slave, to now a prisoner in an Egyptian prison. However, despite the circumstances the Lord still watched over Joseph and helped him find favor in the eyes of the warden. In a turn of events similar to what happened in Potiphar's house, "the warden put Joseph in charge of all those held in prison, and he was made responsible for all that was done there. The warden paid no attention to anything under Joseph's care because the LORD was with Joseph and gave him success in whatever he did" (vv. 22–23).

We don't know how long Joseph languished in prison, but after some time he caught a break. Two of Pharaoh's officials, a baker and his cupbearer, were sentenced to prison and came under Joseph's care. While in prison both men had disturbing, vivid dreams. In Egyptian culture at the time it was believed that some dreams could be prophetic, and so the two officials searched for someone to help interpret their visions. Joseph heard of the dilemma and told them that God could expose the meaning of the dreams. When they related the content of their visions God revealed, through Joseph, that in three days the cupbearer would be restored to his former position but the baker would be executed. Joseph told the cupbearer that he (Joseph) had been wrongly imprisoned and begged him to use his proximity to Pharaoh to plead for a pardon.

Three days later things came to pass exactly as predicted; the baker was hanged and the cupbearer returned to his previous duties. Whether he was uncaring, ungrateful, or just so excited to be out of prison that he forgot his promise, the cupbearer did not bring word of Joseph's plight to Pharaoh. Joseph was left again to wait, apparently forgotten by God and man, in the Egyptian prison.

Two years later Pharaoh, ruler of all Egypt, was troubled by a dream. It had been so realistic and disturbing that he summoned all his magicians and wise men to ask them to interpret the meaning of his vision. The following is the account of his dream:

> When two full years had passed, Pharaoh had a dream: He was standing by the Nile, when out of the river there came up seven cows, sleek and fat, and they grazed among the reeds. After them, seven other cows, ugly and gaunt, came up out of the Nile and stood beside those on the riverbank. And the cows that were ugly and gaunt ate up the seven sleek, fat cows. Then Pharaoh woke up.
>
> He fell asleep again and had a second dream: Seven heads of grain, healthy and good, were growing on a single stalk. After them, seven other heads of

grain sprouted—thin and scorched by the east wind. The thin heads of grain swallowed up the seven healthy, full heads. Then Pharaoh woke up; it had been a dream. (Gen. 41:1–7)

No one was able to tell Pharaoh what the dream meant. The cupbearer heard of the dream, belatedly remembered Joseph, and told Pharaoh that Joseph could interpret the dream. Joseph was quickly cleaned up and brought before the ruler. After informing Pharaoh that it was God, not Joseph, who supplied the interpretation, he proceeded to tell what the dream meant.

> Then Joseph said to Pharaoh, "The dreams of Pharaoh are one; God has revealed to Pharaoh what he is about to do. The seven good cows are seven years, and the seven good ears are seven years; the dreams are one. The seven lean and ugly cows that came up after them are seven years, and the seven empty ears blighted by the east wind are also seven years of famine. It is as I told Pharaoh; God has shown to Pharaoh what he is about to do. There will come seven years of great plenty throughout all the land of Egypt, but after them there will arise seven years of famine, and all the plenty will be forgotten in the land of Egypt. The famine will consume the land, and the plenty will be unknown in the land by reason of the famine that will follow, for it will be very severe. And the doubling of Pharaoh's dream means that the thing is fixed by God, and God will shortly bring it about. Now therefore let Pharaoh select a discerning and wise man, and set him over the land of Egypt. Let Pharaoh proceed to appoint overseers over the land and take one-fifth of the produce of the land of Egypt during the seven plentiful years. And let them gather all the food of these good years that are coming and store up grain under the authority of Pharaoh for food in the cities, and let them keep it. That food shall be a reserve for the land against the seven years of famine that are to occur in the land of Egypt, so that the land may not perish through the famine." (Gen. 41:25–36 ESV)

Pharaoh was extremely impressed with Joseph, enough so that he put him in charge of managing the collection and storage of grain that Joseph had proposed. In fact, Joseph was elevated to second-in-command of the entire country, answerable only to Pharaoh himself. Led by God, Joseph guided the country of Egypt through the seven years of plenty and prepared it well for the famine. Grain was stored in abundance so that Egypt had food to spare during the harsh years of drought and hunger.

The rest of the world was not so lucky. Joseph's father and brothers, living in Canaan, ran out of food for their families. Hearing that Egypt had a surplus, Jacob sent his remaining sons to Egypt to buy food. He tried to keep back his youngest son Benjamin, the only other child that his beloved Rachel had given him before she died, but was eventually forced to send him too.

When the band of brothers showed up in Egypt, they were brought into the presence of Joseph. They did not recognize their brother after so many years apart, but he immediately knew who they were. At last he was in a position to take revenge for the suffering that they had put him through.

Joseph, however, had mercy on his brothers. Without revealing his identity to them, he tested them to see if they were willing to put their younger brother Benjamin in harm's way to get the food they needed. He accused Benjamin of stealing Egyptian silver and demanded that they leave him in Egypt as a prisoner. When his brother Judah offered to trade his own life for Benjamin's, Joseph was so moved that he could not continue the charade. Breaking down and weeping, he revealed his true identity and embraced his brothers. He insisted that they bring all their families and his father Jacob to live in Egypt under Joseph's protection. And so the fledgling Israelite nation moved to Egypt and Jacob was reunited with his long-lost son Joseph. The entire Israelite family (and eventual nation) lived in Egypt as honored guests of the Pharaoh.

SO WHAT?

Wow. That is a long, convoluted story. And yet, this entire story sheds light on the truth of Jesus's claims. After wading through all that drama, you may be asking yourself, how in the world does this have anything to do with the Jesus of the New Testament? At first glance, the stories do not seem to have much in common. However, a deeper look at the two narratives show some surprisingly specific similarities. Is that really possible? Consider these points:

1. Jacob had many sons, most of them from three different women. Joseph, for quite some time the only son of Jacob's beloved wife Rachel, was uniquely special to his father. As such, he had an obvious symbol of his status—an extravagant coat that made it clear at a glance that he was different from everyone around him. The ornate robe and the status it signified led to a rift in the family, with the sons of Jacob's other wives hating Joseph enough to eventually consider killing him.

   In the New Testament God is presented as the father of the whole world, including people of every race. Jesus taught that God was both his father and ours. However, Jesus is called his only begotten, or beloved, son in John 3:16 and again at his baptism in Matthew 3:17. As such, he was given the Holy Spirit, a clear symbol of both his authority and his special relationship with God. It gave him the ability to perform miracles that would set him apart from everyone else on earth and cause enmity between him and the ruling religious class of his day.

2. In the Old Testament, Joseph was at home with his father when Jacob sent him out into the world to check on his brothers. His brothers, the forefathers of the entire Jewish nation, hated Joseph so much that they seized him, threw him into a pit, and eventually sold him into the hands of Egypt, the most powerful nation in the world at that time.

In the New Testament, God sent Jesus from heaven to earth as a messenger to his brothers, God's children on earth. The leaders of the Jewish nation hated Jesus so much that they seized him and turned him over to the Romans, the most powerful nation in the world at that time.

3. In Egypt, Joseph served Potiphar, an Egyptian official. Joseph was blameless in managing Potiphar's household but was punished for a crime he did not commit and sentenced to confinement in an Egyptian prison. He remained there for an unknown length of time, which based on Genesis 41:1 seems to have been at least three years.

   Jesus was taken to Pilate and charged with crimes that he did not commit. Although guiltless, he was sentenced to death. Crucified on a Roman cross, he died and was buried in a stone tomb, where his body remained for three days.

4. When he was able to interpret Pharaoh's dream, Joseph was removed from prison and elevated to Pharaoh's right hand as second-in-command of all Egypt.

   Jesus rose from the dead and left his tomb after three days. Acts 7:56 reveals that he was taken to heaven, where he sits at God's right hand.

5. When his brothers came to Egypt seeking salvation from the famine that was afflicting their homeland, Joseph forgave them for their role in betraying him into slavery. Joseph used his position of authority to rescue his brothers from Canaan, where the famine was causing widespread starvation and death, and brought them to Egypt, a land where they lived in luxury because of their relation to Joseph.

   Jesus brings his followers, whom Paul describes as his "adopted" brothers (Rom. 8:15), from a land where sin causes the death of everyone who lives there, into a realm of paradise, which they are only able to enter because of their relationship with him.

So, Joseph was sent from his home far away by his father to check on his brothers. Driven to hatred by his favored status they betrayed him to death, or so they thought. Punished though he was righteous, he rose to sit at the right hand of the ruler, forgave his brothers, and used his position of power to bring all God's people into a land where there was no famine or suffering. Sound familiar?

Are there differences between the two? Sure. But looking at the comparison above, it is obvious that the two stories have an uncanny number of striking similarities. How do we account for them?

There are three options. First, it could be a coincidence. While that is a possible explanation, the number and extent of the similarities make it hard to believe that they can be purely a matter of chance. Second, it is possible that the New Testament writers intentionally patterned their accounts after the story from Genesis in order to give them credibility. This explanation is hard to accept for two reasons. There are four separate gospel accounts, although to be fair many people think that Matthew, Mark, and Luke are all based on an earlier unknown work. However, all four gospels were written at different times, and the gospel of John is clearly not based on the other three. So, if the life of Jesus did not *actually* parallel the story of Joseph from Genesis, all four authors would have had to agree to alter details in order to make it seem similar. You could argue that is in fact what occurred but, if so, it seems odd that none of them would have called attention to it in their accounts. While there are clear efforts to tie Jesus's life and work to the Passover narrative in Exodus and to the Son of Man prophecy in the book of Daniel, Joseph is only mentioned once in the New Testament gospels (John 4:5).. If you were going to try and link the two accounts, why wouldn't you call Jesus the "new Joseph," or at least make some reference to the Genesis account?

The final possibility is that the Gospels, in telling the story of Jesus's life, death and resurrection, naturally parallel the account of Joseph because God intended it that way. By leaving a blueprint of the life, death, and ultimate victory of Jesus in a document written anywhere from five hundred to fourteen hundred years before Jesus actually walked the earth, God was calling his shot, so to speak. The Jewish people spent four hundred years between Old and New Testament times waiting for a messiah and savior, but they were all looking for a military priest/king figure, not someone who was going to be killed as a sacrifice. Yet, when you compare the stories of Jesus and Joseph, you find God's plans hidden in a story written hundreds of years earlier.

If the story of Joseph is intended as a preview of the gospel, it is then important for us to ask what other lessons are contained in the narrative. We learn that the ministry and death of Jesus was not an accident or random event that somehow morphed into a personality cult—it was a plan that God had in mind from the beginning of human history. Just like Jacob loved all his flawed, quarreling, imperfect sons, God loved all his children enough to risk his beloved son, Jesus. As stated in John 3:16, "For God so loved the world that he gave his one and only Son, that whoever believes in him shall not perish but have eternal life." Jacob knew there was risk in sending Joseph out to check on his brothers, but he did it anyway because of his concern for them. We can take comfort in this story, knowing that God feels the same way about us. If you accept that the story of Joseph is a preview of the story of Jesus, you understand that God not only knew that Jesus would be killed, but that he *intended* for his beloved son to die. That is how much He loves each of us, as imperfect as we are. Finally, just like Joseph was happy to welcome his brothers into the land of Egypt even though they had not treated him well at all, Jesus welcomes everyone regardless of their past actions. No one who puts their faith in Christ will be turned away, no matter what they have done previously.

Should you believe that the historical Jesus was actually a spiritual being who was raised from the dead, on the basis of this story? Is it a coincidence that reaches across hundreds of years, or is it a prediction of things to come, hidden like an Easter egg in an ancient text? You may think that this seems like a stretch, but perhaps it is enough of a reason to investigate further. In the chapters to come, we will look at several other narratives from the Old Testament that further illuminate the mission of Jesus.

Chapter 2

The Passover Lamb— Sacrifice and Salvation

Exodus 1–12

WHILE JESUS NEVER MADE any overt attempt to identify himself with Joseph, he went to great lengths to connect his mission on earth with the story of the Passover lamb. The story comes from the second book of the Old Testament, Exodus. The first book of the Old Testament, Genesis, told of the origin of the Israelite nation and ended with Joseph bringing the remnants of his family to safety in Egypt, as discussed in the last chapter. Exodus picks up the story from there, starting with a dramatic shift in the fortunes of the Hebrew nation.

> Then Joseph died, and all his brothers and all that generation. But the people of Israel were fruitful and increased greatly; they multiplied and grew exceedingly strong, so that the land was filled with them.
>
> Now there arose a new king over Egypt, who did not know Joseph. And he said to his people, "Behold, the people of Israel are too many and too mighty for us. Come, let us deal shrewdly with them, lest they multiply, and, if war breaks out, they join our enemies and fight

against us and escape from the land." Therefore they set
taskmasters over them to afflict them with heavy burdens. They built for Pharaoh store cities, Pithom and
Raamses. But the more they were oppressed, the more
they multiplied and the more they spread abroad. And
the Egyptians were in dread of the people of Israel. So
they ruthlessly made the people of Israel work as slaves
and made their lives bitter with hard service, in mortar
and brick, and in all kinds of work in the field. In all their
work they ruthlessly made them work as slaves. (Ex.
1:6–14 ESV)

In a sense, the Israelites were victims of their own success.
They grew strong and prosperous enough that the native Egyptians were afraid of them. They made the Israelites into a nation of
slaves and worked them to exhaustion. As revealed later in the first
chapter of Exodus, Pharaoh wasn't convinced that he had done
enough to quash this upstart nation. He ordered all male Hebrew
babies to be put to death, in an effort to keep the population under
control.

It is into this tragic story that one of the most famous characters in the Bible and maybe all of history is introduced. The second
chapter of Exodus tells us that a baby boy was born to a man and
woman of the Levite tribe. They hid him from the Egyptians for
three months to spare his life, but eventually could conceal him no
longer. The mother took a basket, coated it with pitch, and placed
her child in it before hiding it among the reeds by the bank of the
Nile River. The boy's older sister stayed close by, watching to see
what would happen.

Soon after, the daughter of Pharaoh came down to the river
to bathe and noticed the basket among the reeds. Opening the basket, she saw the baby crying and was filled with compassion. Even
though she recognized it as one of the Hebrews' children, she took
the baby into Pharaoh's palace and raised it as her own. She named
the baby Moses.

In contrast with his relatives, Moses enjoyed a life of privilege as he grew up in Pharaoh's house. However, he still identified

closely with his fellow Israelites. The following account is found in the second chapter of Exodus:

> One day, when Moses had grown up, he went out to his people and looked on their burdens, and he saw an Egyptian beating a Hebrew, one of his people. He looked this way and that, and seeing no one, he struck down the Egyptian and hid him in the sand. When he went out the next day, behold, two Hebrews were struggling together. And he said to the man in the wrong, "Why do you strike your companion?" He answered, "Who made you a prince and a judge over us? Do you mean to kill me as you killed the Egyptian?" Then Moses was afraid, and thought, "Surely the thing is known." When Pharaoh heard of it, he sought to kill Moses. But Moses fled from Pharaoh and stayed in the land of Midian. (Ex. 2:11–15 ESV)

Moses, in attempting to rescue one of "his people" from a beating at the hands of an Egyptian, killed the oppressor. As his action became common knowledge, Pharaoh tried to have Moses killed. Moses fled to Midian, a desert wasteland where he would spend the next forty years as a shepherd. I am sure that several times during that forty-year period Moses looked back on his previous life of luxury and compared it to his current spartan existence. Did he regret saving his countryman? Was he satisfied that he did the right thing, happy to sacrifice all he had to save a life?

While no one knows exactly how he felt about his past, we do know what he would have done if given a chance to do it again on a much larger scale. We know because in the next chapter of Exodus we are told of a meeting between God and Moses where God gives him just such an opportunity.

> Now Moses was keeping the flock of his father-in-law, Jethro, the priest of Midian, and he led his flock to the west side of the wilderness and came to Horeb, the mountain of God. And the angel of the LORD appeared to him in a flame of fire out of the midst of a bush. He looked, and behold, the bush was burning, yet it was not consumed. And Moses said, "I will turn aside to see this great sight,

why the bush is not burned." When the LORD saw that he turned aside to see, God called to him out of the bush, "Moses, Moses!" And he said, "Here I am." Then he said, "Do not come near; take your sandals off your feet, for the place on which you are standing is holy ground." And he said, "I am the God of your father, the God of Abraham, the God of Isaac, and the God of Jacob." And Moses hid his face, for he was afraid to look at God.

Then the LORD said, "I have surely seen the affliction of my people who are in Egypt and have heard their cry because of their taskmasters. I know their sufferings, and I have come down to deliver them out of the hand of the Egyptians and to bring them up out of that land to a good and broad land, a land flowing with milk and honey, to the place of the Canaanites, the Hittites, the Amorites, the Perizzites, the Hivites, and the Jebusites. And now, behold, the cry of the people of Israel has come to me, and I have also seen the oppression with which the Egyptians oppress them. Come, I will send you to Pharaoh that you may bring my people, the children of Israel, out of Egypt." (Ex. 3:1–10 ESV)

So, instead of saving just one of his countrymen, Moses was now given the opportunity to save his entire nation. Would he jump at the chance to be back in the limelight, eager to be the savior of his people? His response to God revealed a change of heart.

But Moses said to God, "Who am I that I should go to Pharaoh and bring the children of Israel out of Egypt?" He [God] said, "But I will be with you, and this shall be the sign for you, that I have sent you: when you have brought the people out of Egypt, you shall serve God on this mountain." (Ex. 3:11–12 ESV)

Moses, once the "hot stuff" of the Hebrews, living in Pharaoh's palace, now asked God, "Who am I that I should go?" Forty years of a nomadic, anonymous existence in the wilderness sapped his confidence. Or maybe he remembered what happened the last time he bucked the system. In any case, God's response would, to me at least, not have been too comforting: "this shall be a sign for you, that I have sent you: when you have brought the people out of Egypt, you shall serve God on this mountain." Oh, so *after* I do the super-dangerous part of the job you will give me a sign that you're really with me. I don't think that I would have been reassured much by that promise. Moses apparently felt the same. In the third and fourth chapters of Exodus, he responds to God's command with the following variety of excuses:

> Then Moses said to God, "If I come to the people of Israel and say to them, 'The God of your fathers has sent me to you,' and they ask me, 'What is his name?' what shall I say to them?" (Ex. 3:13 ESV)
> Then Moses answered, "But behold, they will not believe me or listen to my voice, for they will say, 'The LORD did not appear to you.'" (Ex. 4:1 ESV)
> But Moses said to the LORD, "Oh, my Lord, I am not eloquent, either in the past or since you have spoken to your servant, but I am slow of speech and of tongue." (Ex. 4:10 ESV)
> But he said, "Oh, my Lord, please send someone else." (Ex. 4:13 ESV)

Moses was able to come up with a million reasons/excuses why he was not the man for the job, so much so that finally "the LORD's anger burned against Moses" (Ex. 4:14). God gave Moses the ability to perform specific miraculous signs to convince the Israelite leaders of his divine ordination, and also assigned Moses's brother Aaron to go with him as his spokesperson. With his excuses exhausted, Moses headed back to Egypt to tell Pharaoh, "Let my people go."

Perhaps predictably, things didn't go well. Moses met Pharaoh and told him that the people of Israel needed to travel into the wilderness for three days in order to have a feast and sacrifice to their God. Pharaoh decided that the Hebrews were lazy and that wanting to take a break for a feast was a sign that they didn't have enough to do. So he told his foremen, "You shall no longer give the people straw to make bricks, as in the past; let them go and gather straw for themselves. But the number of bricks that they made in the past you shall impose on them, you shall by no means reduce it, for they are idle. Therefore they cry, 'Let us go and offer sacrifice to our God.' Let heavier work be laid on the men that they may labor at it and pay no regard to lying words" (Ex. 5:7–9 ESV).

Naturally the Israelites, now having to work harder than ever, were not big fans of Moses and Aaron. They met the two of them and said, "The LORD look on you and judge, because you have made us stink in the sight of Pharaoh and his servants, and have put a sword in their hand to kill us" (Ex. 5:20–21 ESV).

You have to feel a little sorry for Moses at this point. After all, he did (*very* reluctantly) take on a difficult job he didn't want to do, and now everybody was mad at him. The Israelites likely viewed him as someone who got special treatment living in Pharaoh's palace for forty years who had now returned to stick his nose in where it didn't belong and make their lives harder. The Egyptians probably saw him as a renegade who repaid the privilege they gave him by killing one of his benefactors and was now back to cause even more trouble. He must have longed for the simple, uncomplicated routine of raising sheep in the wilderness. At this low point in his life, God stepped up with more concrete signs of his support for Moses.

Over the next few months the Egyptian nation was struck with a series of ten plagues from God in order to convince Pharaoh to let the Israelites leave. The story of the first nine plagues is told in the seventh through the tenth chapters of Exodus and makes very interesting reading if you have the time to peruse it. I will briefly summarize the account here before moving on to the tenth plague, the focus of this chapter.

At first the water in the Nile River was turned to blood. Then Egypt faced successive swarms of frogs, gnats, and flies that completely overran the entire country. After that, a plague on the livestock caused most or all of the donkeys, camels, and other flocks of the Egyptians to die. This was followed by an outbreak of disease that caused painful boils to erupt on the Egyptian people, and then by a hailstorm that destroyed the crops in the fields of Egypt, along with killing any remaining livestock outside.

Following the onset of each plague, Pharaoh would ask Moses to intercede with God to have the plague end, promising to release the people as soon as it did. Each time, as soon as the plague was over, he would change his mind and renege on his promise. After the seventh plague had devastated the country, his counselors begged him, "Let the men go, that they may serve the LORD their God. Do you not yet understand that Egypt is ruined?" (Ex. 10:7 ESV).

Perhaps Pharaoh's pride was just too much for him to swallow, or perhaps, as indicated in the text, God played a part in his resistance. For whatever reason, Pharaoh looked out over the desolation of his once mighty nation and decided that he would try to ride this one out just a little longer. He offered to let Moses take the people, but only if they left their children behind. This, of course, was unacceptable and the plagues continued. Next, a swarm of locusts descended on Egypt, a swarm so massive that the land was darkened. Every green plant that had escaped the previous plagues was quickly devoured. As before, Pharaoh quickly repented, but once the locusts were gone he returned to his intransigence. Moses stretched out his hand to heaven, instigating the ninth plague, the descent of darkness onto the land of Egypt for three days. This was not a twilight darkness but a darkness so thick that it could be felt. No one in Egypt was able to move, conduct business, or see each other for the duration of the darkness. In a scene that had to be getting old for Moses (and the other Egyptians), Pharaoh repented and gave Moses permission to go, but only if they left their flocks and herds.

At this point the Lord revealed the substance of the last plague to Moses, which he passed on to Pharaoh. This final plague would be the most devastating of all and would finally break the resistance of the stubborn ruler.

> So Moses said, "Thus says the LORD: 'About midnight I will go out in the midst of Egypt, and every firstborn in the land of Egypt shall die, from the firstborn of Pharaoh who sits on his throne, even to the firstborn of the slave girl who is behind the handmill, and all the firstborn of

the cattle. There shall be a great cry throughout all the land of Egypt, such as there has never been, nor ever will be again. But not a dog shall growl against any of the people of Israel, either man or beast, that you may know that the Lord makes a distinction between Egypt and Israel.' And all these your servants shall come down to me and bow down to me, saying, 'Get out, you and all the people who follow you.' And after that I will go out." And he went out from Pharaoh in hot anger. (Ex. 11:4–8 ESV)

To modern readers this plague is, understandably, hard to reconcile with a merciful and loving God. While the point of this chapter is not to discuss the philosophical implications of suffering caused by God, it is important to note that the Egyptian people had brutally enslaved the Israelites for four hundred years and stood by idly while all the male Hebrews babies were put to death. But for now I want to focus on the statement made by God that He would make a distinction between Egypt and Israel and to look into how that distinction played out.

The Israelites were not automatically exempted from this plague by their nationality, as they had been from some of the previous occurrences. The Lord gave Moses specific instructions to give to the people, as recorded in Exodus 12:1–13 (ESV):

The LORD said to Moses and Aaron in the land of Egypt, "This month shall be for you the beginning of months. It shall be the first month of the year for you. Tell all the congregation of Israel that on the tenth day of this month every man shall take a lamb according to their fathers' houses, a lamb for a household. And if the household is too small for a lamb, then he and his nearest neighbor shall take according to the number of persons; according to what each can eat you shall make your count for the lamb. Your lamb shall be without blemish, a male a year old. You may take it from the sheep or from the goats, and you shall keep it until the fourteenth day of this month, when the whole assembly of the congregation of Israel shall kill their lambs at twilight.

"Then they shall take some of the blood and put it on the two doorposts and the lintel of the houses in which they eat it. They shall eat the flesh that night, roasted on the fire; with unleavened bread and bitter herbs they shall eat it. Do not eat any of it raw or boiled in water, but roasted, its head with its legs and its inner parts. And you shall let none of it remain until the morning; anything that remains until the morning you shall burn. In this manner you shall eat it: with your belt fastened, your sandals on your feet, and your staff in your hand. And you shall eat it in haste. It is the LORD's Passover. For I will pass through the land of Egypt that night, and I will strike all the firstborn in the land of Egypt, both man and beast; and on all the gods of Egypt I will execute judgments: I am the LORD. The blood shall be a sign for you, on the houses where you are. And when I see the blood, I will pass over you, and no plague will befall you to destroy you, when I strike the land of Egypt."

Moses dutifully passed the command on to the people:

Then Moses called all the elders of Israel and said to them, "Go and select lambs for yourselves according to your clans, and kill the Passover lamb. Take a bunch of hyssop and dip it in the blood that is in the basin, and touch the lintel and the two doorposts with the blood that is in the basin. None of you shall go out of the door of his house until the morning. For the LORD will pass through to strike the Egyptians, and when he sees the blood on the lintel and on the two doorposts, the Lord will pass over the door and will not allow the destroyer to enter your houses to strike you. You shall observe this rite as a statute for you and for your sons forever. And when you come to the land that the LORD will give you, as he has promised, you shall keep this service. And when your children say to you, 'What do you mean by this service?' you shall say, 'It is the sacrifice of the LORD's Passover, for he passed over the houses of the people of Israel in Egypt, when he struck the Egyptians but spared our houses.'" (Ex. 12:21–27 ESV)

So in order to avoid being struck by the plague, each family had to sacrifice a lamb and put the blood of the lamb on the doorposts of their house. Anyone inside a house marked by the blood of a Passover lamb would be safe. Anyone staying in a house that was not protected by the blood of the lamb would suffer the loss of their firstborn son.

As predicted, at midnight the angel of the Lord passed through the land and struck down the eldest son in every house in Egypt. The grief and terror of the Egyptians was so great that they begged the Israelites to leave that very night, before anything worse happened. The Lord instituted the Passover meal as an annual celebration for the Hebrew nation to commemorate their exodus from Egypt, the land where they were enslaved for 430 years. Each year, families would gather together and eat the meal dressed as if for travel to remind them all of how God had saved their nation.

SO WHAT?

What in the world does all this have to do with Jesus? Well, it is easy to draw similarities between this narrative and Jesus because the gospel writers and Jesus himself clearly made an effort to identify Christ as the Passover Lamb of the new covenant. Early on, in the first chapter of the gospel of John, John the Baptist sees Jesus and exclaims, "Look, the Lamb of God, who takes away the sin of the world!" (John 1:29).

In first-century Palestine, a lamb had only three uses: to produce wool, to be eaten as food, or to serve as a sacrifice to atone for sins. So when John identified Christ as a lamb who would "take away the sin of the world," he was clearly envisioning him as a lamb to be sacrificed in the same manner as a Passover lamb.

Jesus identified himself as one who would free people from slavery, just as the sacrifice of the Passover lamb led to the Israelites' freedom from Egypt. In John 8:34–36, Jesus said, "Very truly I tell you, everyone who sins is a slave to sin. Now a slave has no permanent place in the family, but a son belongs to it forever. So if the Son sets you free, you will be free indeed."

Finally, and most explicitly, Jesus is identified directly with the Passover lamb on the night before his death while eating the annual Passover meal with his apostles. Luke 22:7–24 contains the story of this final meal, often referred to as the Lord's Supper, which took place immediately before Jesus's arrest and subsequent trial. In those seventeen verses we find the following statements:

> Then came the day of Unleavened Bread, on which the Passover lamb had to be sacrificed. . . . And when the hour came, he reclined at table, and the apostles with him. And he said to them, "I have earnestly desired to eat this Passover with you before I suffer. For I tell you I will not eat it until it is fulfilled in the kingdom of God." . . . And he took a cup, and when he had given thanks he said, "Take this, and divide it among yourselves. . . . And likewise the cup after they had eaten, saying, "This cup that is poured out for you is the new covenant in my blood." (Luke 22:7, 14, 17, 20 ESV)

The parallel account in Matthew's gospel reads, "And he took a cup, and when he had given thanks he gave it to them, saying, 'Drink of it, all of you, for this is my blood of the covenant, which is poured out for many for the forgiveness of sins" (Matt. 26:27–28 ESV).

Jesus, called the Lamb of God, is sacrificed on the same night as the Passover lamb, with the stated intent of pouring out his blood for the forgiveness of many, so that they can be freed from the slavery of sin. It seems pretty clear that in this case Jesus left no doubt that he wanted to be identified with the Passover lamb from Exodus. "Okay," you may say, "you have somewhat heavy-handedly but successfully made that point. So what? Why should I care if Jesus thought he was a second Passover lamb?"

To answer that question, it is important to understand a few critical truths about the Exodus story, as helpfully outlined below.

1. *The Israelites were not saved through the Passover because they were inherently more righteous than the Egyptians.* In fact, if you go on to read the rest of the book of Exodus you will find that shortly after God miraculously saved them from the Egyptian army, almost the entire nation abandoned God to worship an idol made in the shape of a golden calf. The books

of Leviticus and Numbers tell of many other rebellions and constant complaining throughout the wilderness journey of the Hebrews. God became so angry at the Israelites' idolatry and faithlessness that in Exodus 32 he threatened to destroy them altogether; only the intercession of Moses saved the people. So if they were no better than the Egyptians, why were they saved? They were saved through obedience and faith in God. They were told that sacrificing a lamb and placing its blood on their doorposts would save them from the plague of death; those who obeyed were saved. Even the most righteous of the people who did not obey would have suffered the consequences of the plague, while even the most immoral member of the people who obeyed was saved.

The same is true with Jesus. No one is saved from sin through their own righteousness, but only through faith in God's promise and obedience to His word. Likewise, no one is so awful that they are too far from God to be saved. In Mark 2:17, after being criticized for eating with "immoral" people, Jesus said, "It is not the healthy who need a doctor, but the sick. I have not come to call the righteous, but sinners." Jesus was crucified next to two men identified as criminals. They had likely committed repeated acts of violence, a fact acknowledged by one of them when he said, "We are punished justly, for we are getting what our deeds deserve" (Luke 23:41). Yet despite his sinfulness, when he turned to Jesus in faith, that same criminal was told, "Truly I tell you, today you will be with me in paradise" (v. 43). The Passover lambs of the Old and New testaments tell of a salvation available only through obedience based in faith.

2. *The Passover lamb was the only way out of Egypt for the Israelites.* Before the plagues, the Israelites were in a hopeless situation. Egypt was the superpower of the ancient world, and the Hebrews had been enslaved for years and years. They were so weak that the Egyptians could kill the Israelite babies without fear of any sort of uprising or revolt. Without God's intervention they were not going to escape, ever. In

their desperation they cried out to God for relief. When God met Moses at the burning bush to give him his mission, God said, "I have indeed seen the misery of my people in Egypt. I have heard them crying out because of their slave drivers, and I am concerned about their suffering" (Ex. 3:7). When the Israelites cried out to God, he responded to their distress with a plan to save them; those who responded in faithful obedience were rescued.

In John 14:6, Jesus told his followers, "I am the way, and the truth, and the life. No one comes to the Father except through me." Just as the Israelites had only one hope for escape from Egypt, so we have only one way out of the slavery of sin.

3. *The Passover was the basis for a covenant relation between God and His people.* Just as God promised Moses, after the people were rescued from Egypt, they came to worship the Lord on Mount Sinai. There God met them in the form of a cloud that rested on top of the mountain and made a covenant with them. He told Moses, "Thus you shall say to the house of Jacob, and tell the people of Israel: 'You yourselves have seen what I did to the Egyptians, and how I bore you on eagles' wings and brought you to myself. Now therefore, if you will indeed obey my voice and keep my covenant, you shall be my treasured possession among all peoples, for all the earth is mine; and you shall be to me a kingdom of priests and a holy nation'" (Ex. 19:3–6 ESV).

Later, immediately before giving the Ten Commandments, God said, "I am the LORD your God, who brought you out of the land of Egypt, out of the house of slavery" (Ex. 20:2 ESV). He then passed on to Moses the Ten Commandments and the entire law, which the people agreed to keep. It was a covenant relation; they agreed to follow God's law, and in return they would be his chosen people.

The whole relationship was based on their salvation from the land of Egypt. When Christ said, "This cup that is poured out for you is the new covenant in my blood" (Luke

22:20 ESV), he was establishing a new relationship between man and God. As the old covenant was predicated on the rescue of the Israelites via the blood of the Passover lamb, the new covenant would be built on the salvation from sin available to everyone who would avail themselves of the blood of the new Passover lamb. Instead of being restricted to the Hebrew nation, this covenant was open to everyone.

In summary, the Passover and subsequent exodus from Egypt was the seminal event in the foundation of the Israelite nation. Over and over in the Old Testament, when God wanted to remind the nation of his love for them, he referred to himself as the one who brought them out of Egypt with a mighty hand. That salvation was accomplished through the sacrifice of an innocent lamb, whose blood, placed on a doorpost, was a visible sign that the household within trusted the Lord. Just as the story of Joseph validates the truth of Jesus's claim by telling his story before it happened, the story of the Passover lamb is present in the Old Testament to help us understand our plight and to show us the only possible means of escape: a new Passover lamb whose blood is our only hope for salvation from death. In addition, it is another example of the story of Christ being told hundreds of years before it actually happened.

IS THAT ALL?

It may seem that after the events of the Passover, the Israelite nation was home-free. Released from bondage, they were free to go where they pleased and start a new life. Surely after seeing God's power and compassion for their plight, they would gladly follow him to their new home. Unfortunately, things did not go that smoothly for the Jewish nation. Although they had been set free and would be given a clear path to follow, there turned out to be quite a few obstacles left on their way to the Promised Land. In the next chapter we will look at their journey through the wilderness as they traveled to Canaan, the land that God promised to give to Abraham's descendants so many years earlier.

Chapter 3

Joshua—Crossing the River and Coming Back

Exodus 14-17, 19, 32-34; Numbers 10-15

AFTER THE PLAGUE OF the firstborn the Hebrew nation left Egypt en masse. In Exodus 12:37 we are told that six hundred thousand men left, in addition to women and children. Verse 38 states, "Many other people went up with them," indicating that some Egyptians were convinced to follow God by the miracles they had seen. But as it turns out, the leader of Egypt was still not as impressed by the power of the God of the Israelites as he should have been. Shortly after the Passover account, we are told that the minds of Pharaoh and his servants were changed toward the people, and they said, "What is this we have done, that we have let Israel go from serving us?" (Ex. 14:5 ESV).

So they gathered their army and pursued Israel into the wilderness, either as super-optimists or the slowest learners of all time. They soon trapped the fugitive nation against the shores of the Red Sea, but in one of the most famous stories of all time, God parted the waters of the Red Sea and let Israel pass through safely. Pharaoh, the leader of a nation devastated by one miraculous plague after another and grieving the loss of his firstborn son, decided to roll the dice one more time and chased Moses and the Israelite people through the parted waters. Somewhat predictably, the waters came crashing back in and the Egyptian army was destroyed.

So the people of Israel, newly liberated from hundreds of years of slavery and witnesses of multiple miraculous acts of salvation by a God who led them to freedom, were now in the wilderness. Surely they now breathed in the morning air with a sense of wonder and promise, eager to see what their loving Lord had in store for them now.

Well, not exactly. Or at least not for very long. While they did have a giant celebration complete with its own song after their victory, the very same chapter of Exodus finds trouble brewing.

The story of the victory celebration and song of Moses are recorded in Exodus 15:1–21. The very next verse (v. 22) reveals that only three days later, the Israelites were unhappy. They could not find any water that was fit to drink in the wilderness. The land they were in is identified as the Desert of Shur, so it probably was hot and arid. We are told that the only water they found was bitter and not fit to drink. As a result, the people began to grumble against Moses. On one hand, it seems somewhat understandable; water is essential to surviving in the desert and three days is a long time to go. On the other hand, the last several weeks of their lives had consisted of God showing them one miraculous event after another in a saga of liberation, so it would have been reasonable to exercise a little faith. In any case, justified or not, they were upset and complaining. Moses cried out to God and God miraculously cleansed the water for them to drink. He then proceeded to lead them to camp at Elim, a place with twelve springs and seventy palm trees, which sounds like a pretty nice place to stay in the desert.

A few short weeks later, the people were at it again. They were now traveling in the Desert of Sin, which sounds like one of the levels of Dante's Inferno. And, much like many of the characters in that book, the Israelites were not happy. Now they were hungry, and they were not shy about telling Moses about it: "Would that we had died by the hand of the LORD in the land of Egypt, when we sat by the meat pots and ate bread to the full, for you have brought us out into this wilderness to kill this whole assembly with hunger" (Ex. 16:3 ESV).

This seems to be a little bit of revisionist history; if you recall from the last chapter, while they were in Egypt all their male babies were killed shortly after being born and they were forced to perform slave labor from dusk until dawn. In fact, things were so bad that they had cried out to the Lord to take them *out* of Egypt. Now, driven by hunger, they had romanticized their time in Egypt as a Norman Rockwell painting, sitting around meat pots and gorging themselves on bread. God again patiently came to the rescue. He caused a bread called manna to appear on the ground every morning, and quail to come to the camp every evening. In this manner the Israelites were fed daily the entire time they were traveling in the wilderness.

After all this, we find the people grumbling *again,* this time about a lack of water. They were so angry that Moses cried out to God, "What am I to do with these people? They are almost ready to stone me!" (Ex. 17:4 ESV). God ordered Moses to strike a rock in the camp with his staff; when he did so, water came gushing out of the rock to provide water for all the people. This story becomes important again later on, but for now it serves to demonstrate the continued rebelliousness of the people Moses led.

So, what is the point of all these repetitive accounts of problems? It is important to understand that the Israelites were not model citizens. The name Israel is a Hebrew word that means "struggles with God," and the Israelites did their best to live up to it. And if all the problems to this point weren't bad enough, things rapidly became worse—much worse. However, before we get to that, a new character is introduced.

Joshua, the focus of our current chapter, appears out of nowhere in Exodus 17:9. Every other major figure in the story of the Jewish nation to this point—Abraham, Isaac, Jacob, Joseph, and Moses—is given a lengthy origin story. Not so with Joshua; he pops up out of nowhere as a general charged with leading the Israelites into battle against the Amalekites. With God's help, the Israelites win the battle and the story proceeds to events that occur at Mount

Sinai, where things really went south. From this point onward Joshua is always present with Moses as his second-in-command.

Finally, after all this wandering and complaining, the people reached Mount Sinai. It was here where they would meet with God in person, so to speak, and establish a lasting covenant with him. Along with the Passover, the subsequent exodus and parting of the Red Sea, the events at Mount Sinai are among the cornerstones in the founding of the Hebrew nation. They arrived there roughly three months after departing Egypt. It was here that God communicated to Moses His plan to make Israel a consecrated nation.

> There Israel encamped before the mountain, while Moses went up to God. The LORD called to him out of the mountain, saying, "Thus you shall say to the house of Jacob, and tell the people of Israel: 'You yourselves have seen what I did to the Egyptians, and how I bore you on eagles' wings and brought you to myself. Now therefore, if you will indeed obey my voice and keep my covenant, you shall be my treasured possession among all peoples, for all the earth is mine; and you shall be to me a kingdom of priests and a holy nation.' These are the words that you shall speak to the people of Israel." (Ex. 19:2–6 ESV)

The people expressed their agreement to Moses and were ordered to spend two days consecrating themselves before meeting with the Lord. On the third day they gathered at the foot of the mountain. The presence of the Lord descended on the mountain in awe-inspiring fashion, as described in Exodus 19:16–20 (ESV):

> On the morning of the third day there were thunders and lightnings and a thick cloud on the mountain and a very loud trumpet blast, so that all the people in the camp trembled. Then Moses brought the people out of the camp to meet God, and they took their stand at the foot of the mountain. Now Mount Sinai was wrapped in smoke because the LORD had descended on it in fire. The smoke of it went up like the smoke of a kiln, and the whole mountain trembled greatly. And as the sound of the trumpet grew louder and louder, Moses spoke, and

God answered him in thunder. The LORD came down on
Mount Sinai, to the top of the mountain. And the LORD
called Moses to the top of the mountain, and Moses went
up.

It is hard to imagine the scene—the top of the mountain
wreathed in flame with smoke billowing upward, a trumpet blast
growing louder and louder, and the whole mountain shaking. The
people were terrified, as I am sure I would have been. They pleaded
with Moses not to have God speak to them directly, for fear that
they would not survive it. And so Moses went up on the mountain
to meet with God while the people remained at a distance.

The plan at this point was to have God deliver his law to
Moses, the law that the Israelites had agreed to keep as their part
of the covenant: "if you will indeed obey my voice and keep my
covenant, you shall be my treasured possession" (Ex. 19:5 ESV). As
mentioned above, the people were so terrified by the appearance
of God and the thunder of his voice that they elected to stay back
while Moses went up on the mountain to receive the Law. Unfortunately, there was a lot of law to record, and Moses was on the
mountain for forty days and forty nights—a very long time. Surely
the Israelites, encamped within sight of the awesome image of the
presence of God on the mountain, could spend that long without
getting into trouble, right? Uh, no. Exodus 32 tells the sad story:

> When the people saw that Moses delayed to come down
> from the mountain, the people gathered themselves
> together to Aaron and said to him, "Up, make us gods
> who shall go before us. As for this Moses, the man who
> brought us up out of the land of Egypt, we do not know
> what has become of him." So Aaron said to them, "Take
> off the rings of gold that are in the ears of your wives,
> your sons, and your daughters, and bring them to me."
> So all the people took off the rings of gold that were in
> their ears and brought them to Aaron. And he received
> the gold from their hand and fashioned it with a graving
> tool and made a golden calf. And they said, "These are
> your gods, O Israel, who brought you up out of the land

of Egypt!" When Aaron saw this, he built an altar before it. (Ex. 32:1–5, ESV)

So, here is this nation of former slaves, all of whom have seen wonders and miracles piled on top of each other for months in a row as they escape Egypt. Within sight of their camp is a mountain crowned with thick darkness, lightning, and thunder, and they are less than two weeks removed from crying out in agreement to be God's covenant nation. After all that, it only takes forty days or less for them to abandon God and build an idol. As Joshua and Moses descend the mountain with the law of God written on two stone tablets, they hear a loud noise rising from the camp. Joshua, alarmed, thinks that they have been attacked, saying to Moses that there is the sound of war in the camp. Moses, who either has better hearing or at this point is more familiar with the nature of the people he leads, replies, "It is not the sound of victory, it is not the sound of defeat; it is the sound of singing that I hear" (v. 18).

Entering the camp, they find the idolatrous celebration in full swing. Joshua's response is not recorded but Moses is so angry that he dashes the stone tablets containing the Law onto the ground, shattering them into pieces. What follows next is familiar to anyone who has come home to find their kids standing in the middle of broken furniture or an unauthorized party; there is a lot of finger-pointing and blame-shifting. God is so fed up with the Israelites that he threatens to destroy them and start over. Moses destroys the calf by burning it and making the people drink the ashes, and he himself is required to return to the mountain and make new stone tablets to replace the ones he broke. The people, chastised, renew their covenant with God and Moses instructs them to build a tabernacle, or large tent, that will serve as the mobile center of worship for them while they travel through the desert. Moses would go to the tabernacle to meet with God, and we are told that when "Moses would return to the camp . . . his young aide Joshua son of Nun did not leave the tent" (Ex. 33:11).

So to make a long story short(ish), this would happen over and over again as the Israelites travel through the wilderness—wash, rinse, repeat. The people complain or rebel against God;

God punishes them; and they repent for a while. Specific episodes are recorded Numbers 11–12, 16, 20–21 if you want to look them up. Finally, though, after many months, the people arrived at the Jordan River, the last barrier to cross before they reached Canaan. God had promised them that Canaan, a land "flowing with milk and honey" (Num. 14:8), would be given to them as an inheritance and that he would go with them to establish their residence there. As they camped on the banks of the Jordan, Moses chose twelve men—one from each tribe—to go across and spy out the land in order to help them prepare for their invasion. The representative from the tribe of Ephraim was Joshua.

What did the spies find? The results were mixed. On the one hand, the land itself was amazing, just as God had predicted. We are told that they cut down a single branch with a cluster of grapes so big that they had to carry it on a pole suspended between two of the men. They also found figs and pomegranates—apparently Canaan was like the Whole Foods of the ancient world. Not all of the news was good, however. The majority of the spies were disheartened.

> Then the men who had gone up with him said, "We are not able to go up against the people, for they are stronger than we are." So they brought to the people of Israel a bad report of the land that they had spied out, saying, "The land, through which we have gone to spy it out, is a land that devours its inhabitants, and the people that we saw in it are of great height. And there we saw the Nephilim (the sons of Anak, who come from the Nephilim), and we seemed to ourselves like grasshoppers, and so we seemed to them." (Num. 13:31–33 ESV)

Of the twelve spies who crossed over the Jordan and returned, only two tried to encourage the people to proceed: Joshua and a man named Caleb, from the tribe of Judah.

> Joshua the son of Nun and Caleb the son of Jephunneh, who were among those who had spied out the land, tore their clothes and said to all the congregation of the people of Israel, "The land, which we passed through to spy

it out, is an exceedingly good land. If the LORD delights in us, he will bring us into this land and give it to us, a land that flows with milk and honey. Only do not rebel against the LORD. And do not fear the people of the land, for they are bread for us. Their protection is removed from them, and the LORD is with us; do not fear them." (Num. 14:6–9 ESV)

So here Israel sat, at the end of their journey, literally within sight of their goal. They had two reports, one pretty discouraging and one urging them to trust the Lord. What would they decide? On the one hand, they had seen God deliver them from impossible situations over and over again; it is likely that they were less than a year or two removed from the exodus and the subsequent parting of the Red Sea. On the other hand, despite multiple examples of God's protection, they seemed to have abandoned or mistrusted him at almost every possible opportunity. Unfortunately, their fears and doubts won out again. Their response is recorded in Numbers 14:1–3 (ESV):

Then all the congregation raised a loud cry, and the people wept that night. And all the people of Israel grumbled against Moses and Aaron. The whole congregation said to them, "Would that we had died in the land of Egypt! Or would that we had died in this wilderness! Why is the LORD bringing us into this land, to fall by the sword? Our wives and our little ones will become a prey. Would it not be better for us to go back to Egypt?" And they said to one another, "Let us choose a leader and go back to Egypt."

When Joshua and Caleb tried to reason with the people and urged them to trust the Lord, the congregation got ready to stone them. At this point God stepped in. Angry at the people for their chronic idolatry and faithlessness, he declared that they would not be allowed into Canaan but would instead be forced to wander in the wilderness through which they had been traveling. They would be nomads for forty years, until all the people of Israel twenty years and older had passed away—all the adults who had seen the miracles God had done to rescue them from Egypt but still refused to trust him to protect them in Canaan. However, Joshua and Caleb were to be spared for their faith, and after forty years Joshua would lead the remnant of Israel, now faithful, into Canaan and oversee its settlement there.

SO WHAT?

"Fantastic!," you may say. "A long, convoluted, somewhat depressing story. What in the world does it have to do with Jesus?" A comparison of the two narratives shows undeniable evidence of the story of Jesus written hundreds of years before the historical Jesus walked the earth. Let's look at the similarities.

1. *In the Old Testament, Joshua appears out of nowhere*, with no origin story other than "son of Nun." Along with all Egypt he passes through the Red Sea to Mt. Sinai. There he sees a physical manifestation of God.

    Jesus appears in the New Testament with no earthly father. After a mostly uneventful thirty years of life, he begins a ministry. At the beginning of his ministry he is baptized in the Jordan River, where he sees a physical manifestation of God.

    > When all the people were being baptized, Jesus was baptized too. And as he was praying, heaven was opened and the Holy Spirit descended on him in bodily form like a dove. And a voice came from heaven: "You are my Son, whom I love; with you I am well pleased." (Luke 3:21–22)

2. *After leaving Sinai, Joshua, as a general and surrogate of Moses, led the twelve tribes through the wilderness.* The Lord went before them in the form of a pillar of cloud by day and a pillar of fire at night; in this way they were led by the Lord through the wilderness, where they were tempted by hunger and drought. They would eventually be led through the wilderness for forty years.

Jesus had a remarkably similar experience immediately after his baptism:

> Then Jesus was led by the Spirit into the desert to be tempted by the devil. After fasting for forty days and forty nights, he was hungry. The tempter came to him and said, "If you are the Son of God, tell these stones to become bread."
>
> Jesus answered, "It is written, man does not live on bread alone, but on every word that comes from the mouth of God." (Matt. 4:1–4)

Just like Joshua, Jesus was led by the Spirit into the wilderness, to be tempted for forty days.

3. *After an arduous trek through the wilderness Joshua and the people of Israel arrived at the banks of the Jordan River.* Joshua was required by the Law, represented by Moses, to cross the river ahead of the people. He returned to offer all the people of Israel, who had repeatedly turned their backs on God, an opportunity to cross the river and live in the good land that the Lord had prepared for them. All they had to do was believe in the words of Joshua and follow him, in faith, across the river.

Jesus arrived at the shores of death on the cross. He was required by the Law to cross that boundary for the people he led. He returned with a message of hope, telling everyone that they could join him in that land, even if they had previously rejected God. All they had to do was believe in his words and follow him.

So now you are left with the same question that faces everyone who reads these stories of Joseph, Joshua, and others: Are they *really* that similar, or am I trying to fit a square peg into a round hole? That is for you to decide. As with the Joseph narrative, it is also possible that the Gospel stories were written to intentionally align the narrative of Jesus's life with that of Joshua. However, this would require collusion between all the authors and it seems strange that if they went to that much trouble to associate the two that they would not have drawn more attention to the comparison. The name of Old Testament Joshua does not appear in the Gospel narratives.

So, what does it mean? Let's say, for the sake of argument, that you stipulate that the story of Joshua is intended to be a preview of that of Jesus. What can we learn from it? To answer that question it is critical to understand two points, with each point consisting of two parts.

1a) *Moses represented the Law.* Moses went up Mount Sinai to receive the Law from God and came back down bearing the tablets. Moses then regularly met with God in the tabernacle and returned to pass his words on to the people the entire time the nation traveled through the wilderness. In the New Testament the first five books of the Old Testament are often referred to as the Law of Moses because it was so intimately associated with him. The Law governed almost every aspect of the people's lives and instituted a process of sacrifices that took place at the tabernacle. These sacrifices were to atone for the sins that people committed.

1b) *No one—not a single person—was saved by the Law.* As we have seen, the Hebrew nation performed abysmally when it came to keeping God's commandments. Over and over they complained about their circumstances or turned their back on worshiping God in order to participate in the pagan religions around them. As they stood on the banks of the Jordan River, there was no roll call saying, "The following people step forward. You have kept the Law perfectly and have a free pass to go on across." *Even Moses himself,* the physical embodiment of the law and a man who had been blessed to meet with God one-on-one, was denied entrance to the Promised Land because of his sin.

Numbers 20 tells the story. The nation was once again in the wilderness without water and once again complaining about it. Moses went to God, who told him to verbally command a rock in camp to produce a spring of water. Moses, likely fed up and frustrated with his followers, did things his own way.

> "Hear now, you rebels: shall we bring water for you out of this rock?" And Moses lifted up his hand and struck the rock with his staff twice, and water came out abundantly, and the congregation drank, and their livestock. (Num. 20:10–11 ESV)

Moses asks, "Shall *we* bring water for you out of this rock?," implying that he and God together are going to take care of the people. Then, instead of speaking to the rock as instructed, he strikes it twice. I wonder if there were two quick, angry strikes or if there was one dramatic strike followed by a long awkward pause. Did Moses have a stomach-dropping moment after the first strike where nothing happened, realizing his mistake? If so, he didn't try to fix it but struck the rock again, essentially doubling down on his error. God covered his transgression in front of the people by supplying water but had harsh words for Moses afterward.

> And the LORD said to Moses and Aaron, "Because you did not believe in me, to uphold me as holy in the eyes of the people of Israel, therefore you shall not bring this assembly into the land that I have given them." (Num. 20:12 ESV)

So, ultimately, the Law was incapable of saving anybody—even Moses, the man who forever after would be most closely associated with it.

2a) *Joshua represents faith.* When Joshua pleaded with the people of Israel to cross over into the land of Canaan, he did not base his argument on any righteousness that they had attained from following the Law. Instead, he encouraged them to trust God, to put their faith in the one who had protected them ever since they left Egypt. Look again at the words he used in Numbers 14:8–9 (ESV):

> If the LORD delights in us, he will bring us into this land
> and give it to us, a land that flows with milk and honey.
> Only do not rebel against the LORD. And do not fear the
> people of the land, for they are bread for us. Their protec-
> tion is removed from them, and the LORD is with us; do
> not fear them.

Joshua's argument was based solely on trusting in God to take care of them. In contrast to most of the others there (all but eleven), Joshua had actually been across the river and seen the Nephilim, a race of people much larger and stronger than the Israelites. He had looked at the walled cities and armies that were there. It didn't faze him, because he knew that if God was with them it didn't matter what was on the other side.

2b) *Everyone—every single person—can be saved by faith.* Let's face it: by this point in the story the Israelites don't sound like a bunch of winners. They were chronic whiners and complainers who seemed to always want the easy way out. This is encouraging—because so are we most of the time. Even after their chronic backsliding, rebellion, and complaining, as they stand on the banks of the Jordan River, they *all* can cross over. Joshua doesn't divide them into two groups and say, "Look, those guys over there are never going to make it, right? But *you guys* have a chance! You're the A-team! Let's get this going!" Every single person, even the worst of the perpetrators, had an opportunity to speak up and say, "You know what? He's right! Remember what God has done for us! This is what we came here to do, so let's do it!" Only one other person, Caleb, was willing to trust the Lord, and he was the only other adult who had made the trip from Egypt who also made it across the Jordan into the Promised Land.

It is up to you to decide whether there is anything more than coincidence here. As for me, it is clear that God left the story of Joshua to point us to Jesus. And thankfully, that is an incredibly encouraging thought. It means that even when I am as hopeless and as shameless and faithless as the Israelites sometimes were, there is still a path for me into God's promised land. It means that I can look across the river at the dark, terrifying specter of death and take heart because God has already sent someone across. Jesus went and he came back, just like Joshua did for the Israelites. Earlier we read Joshua's report, encouraging the nation of Israel not to be afraid of what was across the Jordan. Jesus also returned from across the river, with a report for those of us on the other side:

> "Let not your hearts be troubled. Believe in God; believe also in me. In my Father's house are many rooms. If it were not so, would I have told you that I go to prepare a place for you? And if I go and prepare a place for you, I will come again and will take you to myself, that where I am you may be also. And you know the way to where I am going." Thomas said to him, "Lord, we do not know where you are going. How can we know the way?" Jesus said to him, "I am the way, and the truth, and the life. No one comes to the Father except through me." (John 14:1–6 ESV)

To sum up: Joshua took over leadership of the Israelite nation after they had wandered through the wilderness, repeatedly failing to live up to God's law under the leadership of Moses. Despite their failures, he gave them all a chance to cross over Jordan into the Promised Land if they would only trust in his words. Similarly, Jesus showed up to lead the Jewish nation after they spent hundreds of years failing to live up to the Law that they had been given; we will examine the extent of their failure in the chapters ahead. Regardless, Jesus offered them, and each of us, a chance to cross over into a better promised land, if we would only trust his teachings. As you listen to the words of Jesus, you have the same choice that the Israelites had thousands of years ago. Trusting requires taking some risks, but putting your faith in him is all that is required to find rest in his promised land, even if your history is full of mistakes.

IS THAT ALL?

At this point, you may be thinking that the Israelites' troubles were at an end. I mean, they made it through the wilderness, across the Jordan River (eventually) and into a land God had prepared for them, a land flowing with milk and honey. What could possibly go wrong? As it turns out, a lot. Or at the very least, some good and some bad. In the next chapter we will cover, briefly, the history of the Hebrew nation in Canaan and the fall from grace that led to one of the most famous stories in the Bible.

Chapter 4

Daniel—The Stone Rolled Away
Daniel 1–2, 6

IF YOU MENTION THE NAME Daniel in regard to the Bible, most people immediately think of the story of Daniel in the lion's den. To really understand the story of Daniel, though, you have to have some knowledge of the history of the Israelite nation following its arrival in the Promised Land. After Moses died, Joshua led the Israelites into Canaan and was largely successful in settling them there through a succession of battles of conquest, a story that is told in the helpfully named book of Joshua. Following that conquest, things did not go great. In a pattern that was to be repeated over and over, the people abandoned God to follow Canaanite religions. Falling away from God always led to oppression that would eventually get bad enough for the people to repent and cry out to God for help. God would raise up warriors to liberate the people from their oppressors, which would lead to a time of faithfulness from the community before falling away again. The story of these years is told in the book of Judges.

After years of this cycle the people of Israel decided that they wanted a king to rule them as a nation. Rather than acknowledge that their issues were the result of not following God, they decided that the surrounding nations were stronger because they had kings. They came to Samuel, who was currently leading Israel, with the demand for a king. He warned them against rejecting God as their king and told them about the hardships that kings would impose on them. The people were adamant, and God told Samuel that he would provide them with a king. Things got off to a little bit of a rocky start with the first king, Saul, but quickly improved. The next two kings, David and his son Solomon, represented the high-water mark of the Old Testament kingdom of Israel. Through conquest and tribute they became the dominant force in the Middle East. Thanks to David's military success, his son Solomon ruled in a time of unprecedented peace and prosperity, and built a magnificent temple in Jerusalem that would function as a focal point for the nation's worship of God.

Unfortunately, things went downhill after that. Solomon became a victim of his own success and began to enjoy the pleasures of the world instead of living according to the Law. The Israelites had been instructed not to marry people from the surrounding cultures to prevent them from being drawn into their religions, but Solomon did so in a big way. First Kings 11:3 tells us that Solomon had *seven hundred wives* and more than *three hundred concubines*. As a result, he began to participate in their idolatry and even built them high places, or shrines, to offer sacrifices.

The Israelites had been unified as a single kingdom up to this point, but following Solomon's death a power struggle led to a split that resulted in a larger northern kingdom and a smaller southern kingdom. This smaller southern kingdom consisted of only two of the original twelve tribes, Judah and Benjamin, but did hold the city of Jerusalem and the temple. Neither kingdom was consistently faithful to God; despite a few righteous kings, mostly in the southern kingdom, the tale of the next two hundred years is one of a mostly downward slide into idolatry, violence, and immorality. Multiple prophets came to the people, warning them of severe consequences if they did not repent and return to the Lord. They were largely ignored, persecuted, or killed. Eventually, the prophecies came true: in 722 BC the Assyrian nation conquered Samaria, the capital city of the northern tribes; and less than 140 years later, in 586 BC, the Babylonian army conquered and sacked Jerusalem, marking the end of the southern kingdom.

After both of these defeats, surviving Israelites were deported to other countries as hostages, to prevent rebellion and to promote assimilation into the cultures of their conquerors. This is where the story of Daniel begins.

Daniel lived in the southern kingdom of Judah. The kingdom had enjoyed a brief religious reform under the rule of King Josiah, one of the more righteous kings in its history. Unfortunately, Josiah was killed in battle with the Egyptians, and sometime around 609 BC Jehoiakim became king and led the nation back into a quagmire of idolatry and sin. The king of Babylon, Nebuchadnezzar, attacked and conquered Jerusalem in 605 BC, taking multiple hostages back to Babylon with him.

One of those hostages was a boy named Daniel, who was likely around fifteen years old at the time. We know a few things about Daniel from the text of the Old Testament book that bears his name. His story begins as follows:

> Then the king commanded Ashpenaz, his chief eunuch, to bring some of the people of Israel, both of the royal family and of the nobility, youths without blemish, of good appearance and skillful in all wisdom, endowed with knowledge, understanding learning, and competent to stand in the king's palace, and to teach them the literature and language of the Chaldeans. (Dan. 1:3–4 ESV)

So Daniel was likely from a well-to-do family, handsome in appearance, and relatively clever. His background and aptitude identified him as a candidate to be trained in the ways of his conquerors so that he could be of service to them. It is easy to imagine how disorienting and frightening it would be to be thrust into that situation. Likely coming from a relatively sheltered background, Daniel was ripped away from everything and everyone he knew and taken to a foreign land with an unfamiliar language and customs. That kind of trauma would naturally lead to all kinds of anxiety, stress, and fear for anyone, and likely much more so for an adolescent on his own. The easy thing to do would certainly be to put your head down, conform, and try not to draw too much attention to yourself in an effort to weather the storm. As we read in the next few verses, Daniel was made of a little sterner stuff.

> The king assigned them a daily portion of the food that the king ate, and of the wine that he drank. They were to be educated for three years, and at the end of that time they were to stand before the king. (Dan. 1:5 ESV)

The young people chosen to be in this group must have felt extremely lucky to be included. The Babylonians were not known for being merciful; the fate of many other Israelites was, in all likelihood, not very pleasant. Not only were these young people spared torture, death, or forced labor, but they were also to be fed the same food and wine the king himself had, surely the best in the land. It would be hard for anyone in that situation not to want to sacrifice almost anything to maintain their position. How did Daniel handle this good fortune?

> But Daniel resolved that he would not defile himself with the king's food, or with the wine that he drank. Therefore he asked the chief of the eunuchs to allow him not to defile himself. (Dan. 1:8 ESV)

It is unclear what exactly Daniel found objectionable about the food given to them. The Law of Moses did have strict dietary requirements about which animals could be eaten and how the meat had to be treated during preparation. Eating food that had been offered to the Babylonian gods may have made it objectionable to him. For whatever reason, Daniel was secure enough in his faith in God that he was willing to lose all the advantages he had been given rather than to transgress the law. The official in charge of the youths liked Daniel, but was afraid that if Daniel did not eat what seemed to be the best food his health would suffer, which could be blamed on the official taking care of him. Daniel proposed a solution.

> Then Daniel said to the steward whom the chief of the eunuchs had assigned over Daniel, Hananiah, Mishael,

and Azariah, "Test your servants for ten days; let us be given vegetables to eat and water to drink. Then let our appearance and the appearance of the youths who eat the king's food be observed by you, and deal with your servants according to what you see." So he listened to them in this matter, and tested them for ten days. At the end of ten days it was seen that they were better in appearance and fatter in flesh than all the youths who ate the king's food. So the steward took away their food and the wine they were to drink, and gave them vegetables. (Dan. 1:11–16 ESV)

Daniel was rewarded for his faith; the official in charge was willing to try the proposed experiment and, sure enough, Daniel and his friends ended up looking better than everyone else. This story, placed at the beginning of the book of Daniel, shows what kind of character he had. Even as a teenager displaced into a hostile, unfamiliar culture he was willing to serve God faithfully, even if it meant losing everything he had.

Daniel went on to finish his three-year training period and became a member of the king's "wise men," a group that included advisors, astrologers, and diviners. Almost immediately though, he found that his position placed him in mortal danger. It all began when Nebuchadnezzar, the powerful king of Babylon, started having vivid, troubling dreams. The story is told in the second chapter of Daniel.

In the second year of the reign of Nebuchadnezzar, Nebuchadnezzar had dreams; his spirit was troubled, and his sleep left him. Then the king commanded that the magicians, the enchanters, the sorcerers, and the Chaldeans be summoned to tell the king his dreams. So they came in and stood before the king. And the king said to them, "I had a dream, and my spirit is troubled to know the dream." Then the Chaldeans said to the king in Aramaic, "O king, live forever! Tell your servants the dream, and we will show the interpretation." The king answered and said to the Chaldeans, "The word from me is firm: if you do not make known to me the dream and its interpretation, you shall be torn limb from limb, and your houses shall be laid in ruins." (Dan. 2:1–5 ESV)

The king was having dreams that were troubling enough that he could not sleep; the original translation says his spirit was "struck," like a hammer hitting an anvil. The dream bothered him so much that "his sleep left him." Kings at that time had a court full of learned advisors and other people, probably similar to psychics, who were supposed to be able to interpret all kinds of dreams and omens. Nebuchadnezzar was not going to make it easy on his court, though; before they could try to interpret the dream, they had to tell him what the dream was. On top of that, if they couldn't they were going to be "torn limb from limb." Yikes!

Naturally, the wise men were not super-happy about the way things were playing out. They told their king that no such thing had ever been asked of anyone by any ruler. Furthermore, only gods could know what someone had dreamed, and there were no gods dwelling in the kingdom at that time. Nebuchadnezzar didn't want to hear it and ordered that all the wise men in the kingdom were to be executed. That included Daniel, who had finished his training at what turned out to be an inopportune time. The job of carrying out the king's orders was given to Arioch, the captain of the guard. When he began to round them all up Daniel asked him, "Why is the decree of the king so urgent?" (v. 15). Arioch explained the situation to Daniel, who quickly requested an audience with the king in order to interpret the dream. This could have been an act of faith or of desperation, because as the subsequent text reveals, Daniel as of yet had no idea what the content or meaning of the dream was. As we read we find that Daniel knew that God had the ability to reveal everything if he so desired.

> Then Daniel went to his house and made the matter known to Hananiah, Mishael, and Azariah, his companions, and told them to seek mercy from the God of heaven concerning this mystery, so that Daniel and his companions might not be destroyed with the rest of the wise men of Babylon. Then the mystery was revealed to

Daniel in a vision of the night. Then Daniel blessed the
God of heaven. (Dan. 2:17–19 ESV)

Daniel was rewarded for his faith and proceeded to reveal the
dream and its meaning to Nebuchadnezzar. The following passage
is a little long but included in its entirety here, because the content
and the meaning of the dream are pertinent to the theme of this
chapter.

> Then Arioch brought in Daniel before the king in haste
> and said thus to him: "I have found among the exiles
> from Judah a man who will make known to the king the
> interpretation." The king declared to Daniel, whose name
> was Belteshazzar, "Are you able to make known to me the
> dream that I have seen and its interpretation?" Daniel
> answered the king and said, "No wise men, enchant-
> ers, magicians, or astrologers can show to the king the
> mystery that the king has asked, but there is a God in
> heaven who reveals mysteries, and he has made known
> to King Nebuchadnezzar what will be in the latter days.
> Your dream and the visions of your head as you lay in
> bed are these: To you, O king, as you lay in bed came
> thoughts of what would be after this, and he who reveals
> mysteries made known to you what is to be. But as for
> me, this mystery has been revealed to me, not because
> of any wisdom that I have more than all the living, but in
> order that the interpretation may be made known to the
> king, and that you may know the thoughts of your mind.
>
> "You saw, O king, and behold, a great image. This
> image, mighty and of exceeding brightness, stood before
> you, and its appearance was frightening. The head of this
> image was of fine gold, its chest and arms of silver, its
> middle and thighs of bronze, its legs of iron, its feet partly
> of iron and partly of clay. As you looked, a stone was cut
> out by no human hand, and it struck the image on its feet
> of iron and clay, and broke them in pieces. Then the iron,
> the clay, the bronze, the silver, and the gold, all together
> were broken in pieces, and became like the chaff of the
> summer threshing floors; and the wind carried them
> away, so that not a trace of them could be found. But the

stone that struck the image became a great mountain and filled the whole earth.

"This was the dream. Now we will tell the king its interpretation. You, O king, the king of kings, to whom the God of heaven has given the kingdom, the power, and the might, and the glory, and into whose hand he has given, wherever they dwell, the children of man, the beasts of the field, and the birds of the heavens, making you rule over them all—you are the head of gold. Another kingdom inferior to you shall arise after you, and yet a third kingdom of bronze, which shall rule over all the earth. And there shall be a fourth kingdom, strong as iron, because iron breaks to pieces and shatters all things. And like iron that crushes, it shall break and crush all these. And as you saw the feet and toes, partly of potter's clay and partly of iron, it shall be a divided kingdom, but some of the firmness of iron shall be in it, just as you saw iron mixed with the soft clay. And as the toes of the feet were partly iron and partly clay, so the kingdom shall be partly strong and partly brittle. As you saw the iron mixed with soft clay, so they will mix with one another in marriage, but they will not hold together, just as iron does not mix with clay. And in the days of those kings the God of heaven will set up a kingdom that shall never be destroyed, nor shall the kingdom be left to another people. It shall break in pieces all these kingdoms and bring them to an end, and it shall stand forever, just as you saw that a stone was cut from a mountain by no human hand, and that it broke in pieces the iron, the bronze, the clay, the silver, and the gold. A great God has made known to the king what shall be after this. The dream is certain, and its interpretation sure." (Dan. 2:25–45 ESV)

There are a couple of things to consider here. First, it should be noted that Daniel was careful to give God all the credit for supplying the meaning of the dream. Although he could have promoted himself to gain favor with the king, his faith kept him humble and loyal to God.

Second, the dream itself is a prophecy, meaning that it predicts future events. At this point it is important to mention that the book of Daniel has a lot of prophecies in it, often containing various symbols that represent different nations. Many of them appear to accurately predict world events over the next several hundred years. In fact, they seem to predict some world events so accurately that many scholars believe that there is no way that they could have been written prior to the events occurring. While it is an interesting argument, it does not have any bearing on our discussion. All that matters to us is the fact that Daniel was unquestionably written before the time of Christ. Since Jesus himself referred to passages in Daniel, the text had to be widely known and distributed well before his birth. So, with that out of the way, on to discussing the dream itself.

Nebuchadnezzar had a dream about a giant statue; the top was made of pure gold and the lower levels were made of progressively less valuable but potentially stronger material. The very lowest level was made of iron and was split at the feet into two portions, one of iron and one of clay. Daniel told Nebuchadnezzar that his kingdom, the Babylonian Empire, was represented by the head of gold. The most common interpretation of the rest of the dream is that the next level, made of silver, represented the Persian Empire, which ruled about two hundred years after displacing the Babylonians. The third level, made of bronze, which Daniel said would "rule over all the earth," is usually identified as the Greek dynasty founded by Alexander the Great, who destroyed the Persian rule and did go on to conquer all the known world at the time. The fourth kingdom, made of iron, which Daniel said would break and crush all the others, is usually identified as the Roman Empire, which represented the most dominant military the world had ever seen. Daniel also predicted that this empire would be divided, which would be consistent with the division of the Roman Empire into an eastern half based in Constantinople and a western half based in Rome.

At this point many skeptics may be saying, "Whoa there, big fella! You're just making stuff up—you could take a dream about a statue and make it say whatever you want! All this prophecy is bogus." I would disagree but fortunately, for our purposes, it doesn't really matter whether or not the dream accurately predicts the succession of power in the ancient Mediterranean world. All that really matters is the last part of the dream—in which a stone, one that "was cut out by no human hand," shattered all the kingdoms represented by the statue and then went on to become a huge mountain that filled the whole earth. The meaning of this part of the dream seems pretty clear: a stone that is cut out by no human hand must come from God. Furthermore, it is going to overcome all the earthly kingdoms in the process of building a kingdom in its own right, one that would fill the whole earth. Daniel was telling Nebuchadnezzar that all the earthly dynasties—*whichever* ones happened to be represented in the dream—would be overcome by a kingdom of divine origin. Most Christians believe that this prophecy refers to the coming of Jesus; some believe that the rock represents the establishment of the church, which has outlived all the other kingdoms and has gone on to fill the entire earth. Others believe it refers to a future event: the return of Jesus a second time. For our discussion, the interpretation of the dream has two relevant points: one, that Daniel predicted the coming of a spiritual "rock" that would destroy all other earthly kingdoms; and two, that because Daniel fervently believed that God was in control of worldly events and would bring that judgment to pass, that he, Daniel, was responsible to a higher power than whatever ruler was currently in charge. It is that principle that plays out in the next episode. It is one of the most famous stories in the Bible and maybe of all time: Daniel in the lion's den.

Nebuchadnezzar was impressed with Daniel's ability to identify and interpret his dream. As a result he placed Daniel in a position of power, putting him in charge of the entire province of Babylon and all its wise men. Daniel served in Nebuchadnezzar's royal court from that day forward. For a while, things went really well. Nebuchadnezzar was, apparently, one of the more impressive rulers of the ancient world, and as long as he was at the helm of the Babylonian Empire it prospered. After he died in 562 BC his magnificent empire only lasted for roughly twenty-three years. In 539 BC Cyrus the Great, king of Persia, conquered the city of Babylon and ended the Neo-Babylonian dynasty. This turn of events is alluded to at the end of Daniel 5: "That very night Belshazzar the Chaldean [Babylonian] king was killed. And Darius the Mede received the kingdom, being about sixty-two years old" (Dan. 5:30–31 ESV).

This has caused some controversy, since the king of Persia at the time was named Cyrus, with a later Persian ruler being named Darius. There is some evidence that the Darius mentioned was the governor of Babylon serving under Cyrus, but historians disagree whether the text is historically accurate or not. You can do a Google search on "Daniel and Darius" and get several different views on both sides of the subject. What matters to our story is that there was a new sheriff in town. By this point Daniel was likely around seventy-five or eighty years old, having lived his whole adult life as a cog in the administrative wheel of a foreign country. His old age did not affect his ability to do his job effectively. Darius was determined to reorganize the government that he had taken over; he divided the area of his rule into 120 districts and placed a governor, or satrap, over each one. He then appointed three higher officials to rule over all of the satraps. One of these three upper-level rulers was none other than Daniel. In fact, Daniel "became distinguished above all the other high officials and satraps, because an excellent spirit was in him" (Dan. 6:3 ESV).

He did such an outstanding job that Darius soon decided to elevate him to a position over the whole kingdom. Naturally, this caused a lot of jealousy among the other officials, and they began to conspire together to find a way to bring Daniel down. However, try as they might, there was nothing sufficiently incriminating that they could uncover. In fact, after all their efforts to sabotage him the group concluded, "We shall not find any ground for complaint against this Daniel unless we find it in connection with the law of his God" (Dan. 6:5 ESV).

With that in mind, the group hatched a plan. They went to Darius and told him, "All the high officials of the kingdom, the prefects and the satraps, the counselors and the governors [were] agreed" that he should pass a law stating that "whoever makes petition to any god or man for thirty days, except to you, O king, shall be cast into the den of lions" (Dan. 6:7 ESV). At first glance this seems like a pretty unusual request. Did it play to the ruler's vanity? Was it related to some religious festival of the Persians, where supplications to foreign gods would be objectionable? No one really knows. But Darius, perhaps persuaded by the supposedly unanimous support of all his underlings, signed the idea into law.

Well, obviously not all of his satraps were on board with the idea. We know that at least Daniel would have never supported the law, but his response to it again confirms his character. Notice that the law was only in effect for thirty days; it didn't state that no one could ever worship another deity. How easy it would have been for Daniel to take a little time off from prayer and then resume his routine after the thirty-day limit had expired. Instead, we are told that after Daniel knew the document had been signed, "he went home to his upstairs room where the windows opened toward Jerusalem. Three times a day he got down on his knees and prayed, giving thanks to his God, just as he had done before" (v. 10). Apparently Daniel prayed from an upstairs room with the windows open so that he could look in the direction of Jerusalem when he talked with God. While he could have simply closed the windows to prevent anyone from seeing him praying, he did not allow the law to affect his routine. It is likely that he had kept the same schedule for the seventy-odd years that he had been exiled. Clearly, his daily conversation with God was an integral component of his faith.

Daniel's enemies must have been familiar with his practice because they wasted no time in gathering witnesses to his prayer and running to Darius with the information. The ruler valued Daniel as a valuable asset and/or as a person, as we are told that "he was greatly distressed; he was determined to rescue Daniel and made every effort until sundown to save him" (v. 14). You can picture the ruler poring over documents and consulting legal experts in a frantic effort to find some loophole that would save his trusted advisor. Unfortunately, all his work was to no avail.

At sunset, the conspirators came to remind him that, once signed into law, there was no changing a decree. Reluctantly Darius summoned Daniel and had him cast into the den of lions. Before leaving him, Darius offered what likely seemed to him a forlorn hope: "May your God, whom you serve continually, deliver you!" (v. 16). With that, a large stone was placed over the opening of the den and sealed with the king's signet ring. The ruler returned to his residence but spent a sleepless night, agonizing over Daniel's fate.

The end of the story is found in Daniel 6:19–24 (ESV):

> Then, at break of day, the king arose and went in haste to the den of lions. As he came near to the den where Daniel was, he cried out in a tone of anguish. The king declared to Daniel, "O Daniel, servant of the living God, has your God, whom you serve continually, been able to deliver you from the lions?" Then Daniel said to the king, "O king, live forever! My God sent his angel and shut the lions' mouths, and they have not harmed me, because I was found blameless before him; and also before you, O king, I have done no harm." Then the king was exceedingly glad, and commanded that Daniel be taken up out of the den. So Daniel was taken up out of the den, and no kind of harm was found on him, because he had trusted in his God. And the king commanded, and those men who had maliciously accused Daniel were brought and cast into the den of lions—they, their children, and their wives. And before they reached the bottom of the den, the lions overpowered them and broke all their bones in pieces.

It seems likely that Darius did not hold out much hope that his call to Daniel on that morning would be answered. But to his joy and surprise he found Daniel alive and unharmed. Removing him from the pit, he took vengeance on the men who had formed the cabal against Daniel in the first place. Daniel likely resumed his role as second-in-command, as we are told that he prospered during the reign of Darius and the reign of Cyrus the Persian.

SO WHAT?

At this point you may be saying, "Sure, that's a great story that I maybe heard in Sunday school a billion years ago, but who cares? What could it possibly have to do with me?" I think that there are two important things to learn from the story of Daniel.

First, like the previous stories that we have looked at, the story of Daniel has too many parallels to the story of Jesus to be coincidental. Consider the following:

1. *Daniel was exiled from Jerusalem, which he calls the "beautiful land" (Dan. 11:16), because of the sinful behavior of the people of Israel.* Although Daniel is not himself sinless, he is presented as a paragon of virtue and faith who is exiled to life in the pagan kingdom of Babylon, then Persia. Jesus left the beautiful land of heaven because of the sin of God's people. While he himself was sinless, he was exiled to the world to atone for the sin of mankind.

2. *Daniel was elevated in the service of the king because of his ability to interpret dreams, his integrity, and because of his faithful service to God.* His rise in popularity resulted in the enmity of the other authorities, who subsequently plotted to have him killed. In Luke 2:52 we are told that as he grew, Jesus "increased in wisdom and in stature and in favor with God and man." His ability to cure illness and perform other miracles resulted in crowds of thousands of followers. His increasing popularity caused jealousy and fear in the Pharisees, scribes, and other religious/social leaders of the day, to the extent that they "went out and immediately held counsel with the Herodians against him, how to destroy him" (Mark 3:6 ESV).

3. *Because of Daniel's personal integrity, his enemies were unable to find any charge against him.* In the end, they had to create a new religious law conflicting with Daniel's personal religious conviction in order to have him sentenced to death.

Jesus's opponents were also unable to find any charge against him. At his trial, we find that "the chief priests and the whole council were seeking testimony against Jesus to put him to death, but found none. For many bore false witness against him, but their testimony did not agree. And some stood up and bore false witness against him, saying, 'We heard him say, "I will destroy this temple that is made with hands, and in three days I will build another, not made with hands."' Yet even about this their testimony did not agree" (Mark 14:55–59 ESV). In the end the only charge that they could bring against him was violation of their religious law: "The Jews answered him, 'We have a law, and according to that law he ought to die because he has made himself the Son of God'" (John 19:7).

4. *Daniel's persecutors did not have the authority to execute him themselves, but had to bring him to a foreign ruler,* possibly a governor appointed to rule in the stead of the Persians. That ruler, Darius, did not want to execute Daniel but labored feverishly to find a way around the punishment. In the end, the conspirators forced his hand: "Know, O king, that it is a law of the Medes and Persians that no injunction or ordinance that the king establishes can be changed" (Dan. 6:15 ESV). Unwilling to break Persian law, Darius relented and allowed Daniel to be cast into the lions' den.

The Jewish leaders had no authority to execute Jesus, but instead took him to Pilate, a governor appointed to rule in the stead of the Roman Empire. Pilate, convinced that Jesus was innocent, repeatedly tried to exonerate him. In John 19:12 (ESV) we are told that "From then on Pilate sought to release him, but the Jews cried out, 'If you release this man, you are not Caesar's friend. Everyone who makes himself a king opposes Caesar.'" Unwilling to cross the Roman Empire, Pilate relented and released Jesus for crucifixion.

5. *Daniel was thrown into the lion's den, a place of certain death.* A stone was placed over the entrance to the den and sealed with the ruler's signet ring.

Jesus was crucified and placed in a tomb cut out of stone. A large stone was rolled into the entrance of the tomb and it was sealed, as we are told in Matthew 27:65–66 (ESV): "Pilate said to them, 'You have a guard of soldiers. Go, make it as secure as you can.' So they went and made the tomb secure by sealing the stone and setting a guard."

6. *Darius rose "at the break of day" and, crying in anguish, went to the lion's den to see what had happened to Daniel.* Upon arrival, he was told that God had sent an angel to rescue Daniel and that Daniel was in fact alive. Daniel was taken out of the den and resumed his place at the ruler's side.

In the New Testament, Mary Magdalene went to the tomb of Jesus, "early, while it was still dark" and "stood weeping outside the tomb" (John 20:1, 11 ESV). There she encountered angels, who told her that Jesus, alive, was no longer in the tomb. Jesus, risen from the dead, would resume his rightful place at his Father's side.

Here we again encounter a story written at least a hundred years and maybe as many as six hundred years before Jesus was born that somehow seems to foretell the events of his life. Is it possible that this many similarities are pure coincidence? Are they truly similar at all, or am I just grasping at straws? The story of Daniel, like those of Joseph and Joshua, is too much like that of Jesus to be coincidence. It seems to be another instance where God, through the writings of the Old Testament, predicted the events that he would set in motion centuries later to reconcile his people to himself.

If so, what can we learn from the story of Daniel that applies to us today? How did he find the courage to face death in the den of lions? Thinking back to the dream of Nebuchadnezzar, Daniel knew he was living in an era dominated by powerful dynasties—kingdoms of gold, silver, and iron that had the power to break men as they pleased. He also knew that something more powerful was coming, a rock not carved by human hands, that was going to crush every earthly kingdom. He was willing to trust his fate to that kingdom, trust that God would prevail over the forces around him. Daniel began this process early in life, at roughly fifteen years of age, risking his position and safety in order to obey the dietary restrictions of the law of Moses. Over the course of his life among the Babylonians and Persians, Daniel's willingness to trust God and God's faithfulness in watching over him culminated in an older man who was willing to go to his death rather than put man's law above God.

Jesus showed the same fortitude and faith. When he was on trial before Pilate, the Roman governor asked him, "Don't you realize that I have the power to free you or to crucify you?" Jesus replied, "You would have no power over me if it were not given to you from above" (John 19:10–11)

He knew that there was a more powerful figure in control, and a coming kingdom that would break the Roman Empire, and he chose to serve it. Likewise his followers, Peter and John, on trial before the Jewish Sanhedrin, said, "Which is right in God's eyes: to listen to you, or to him? You be the judges! As for us, we cannot help speaking about what we have seen and heard" (Acts 4:19–20). They served a more powerful authority than the one who had put them on trial. They were also willing to face death because they knew they were serving a higher kingdom and a higher king.

We have the same choice today. It is hard to go against the powers that be and risk power, prestige, or position to follow God. There is clearly danger involved; although Joseph and Daniel both achieved high-ranking, powerful posts by following God, their faith also led them to prison and the lion's den, respectively. Jesus followed his faith all the way to a painful, humiliating death by crucifixion. How does anyone find the courage to trust God to that extent? I think Daniel gives us at least three answers.

First, start small. Early in life Daniel was willing to lose his position in the king's court in order to follow God's law. Find ways to step out of your comfort zone a little bit at a time. That may mean giving some of your income to God through church, charity, or service and trusting him to provide. It may mean giving up some of your time to reach out and help family members or people in your community who are in need. It may mean not participating in some things that are not in line with a Christian lifestyle. All these things are hard, but you have to step out of your safe zone in order for God to demonstrate that he will take care of you.

Second, start a period of daily prayer. It is telling that when Daniel's enemies wanted to create a law that they knew he would not be able to keep, they banned prayer. It was so critical to Daniel that he risked death rather than stopping it for thirty days. Finding time to pray seems difficult for everybody in today's world but, if you are being honest, most of us have lots of things that seem sacred to us that are not that important. Carve out ten or fifteen minutes every day to talk to God honestly about your worries, problems, and fears. Thank him for the ways that you are blessed. It is much easier to trust someone with whom you are in constant communication.

Third, and finally, look forward to a better kingdom. If everything you care about is in this world then it will be impossible to risk losing it for God. In the sermon on the mount, Jesus said, "Do not store up for yourselves treasures on earth, where moths and vermin destroy, and where thieves break in and steal. But store up for yourselves treasures in heaven, where moths and vermin do not destroy, and where thieves do not break in and steal. For where your treasure is, there your heart will be also" (Matt. 6:19–21).

All the things that we tend to value in this life—wealth, fame, health—can be taken from you in an instant. Jesus taught that there is a much better existence ahead of us, one that can never be taken away. Focusing on it, and not on accumulating power or possessions, will make it easier to risk what you do have in order to serve God.

IS THAT ALL?

So far we have looked at four figures in the Old Testament who heralded the mission of Jesus. Joseph illustrated the story of how Jesus would save his brethren even after they betrayed him to death. The Passover lamb predicted Jesus's sacrifice that would lead God's people out of their slavery to sin. The story of Joshua foretold how Jesus would give us all a chance to cross the river of death into God's chosen land based on faith, instead of our ability to keep the commandments of the law. And, as just discussed, Daniel showed how Christ would trust God to bring him back from death. In the next and final chapter we will look at one of the less famous figures in the Old Testament, a man who was willing to give up everything to rebuild the city of God.

Chapter 5

Nehemiah—Laying the Cornerstone
Nehemiah 1–6, 8–9, 13

THE STORY OF NEHEMIAH, like that of Daniel, is that of an Israelite exile living in the Persian Empire. To truly understand the story of Nehemiah, though, you have to understand the heights from which the kingdom of Israel had fallen.

Israel reached the peak of its power and glory under King Solomon, who ruled around 960 BC. Solomon's father David had conquered the surrounding nations, and so Solomon's reign was a time of peace and prosperity. He built the temple, a building roughly ninety feet long, thirty feet wide, and forty-five feet tall. The inside was covered in pure gold, with an internal room called the Most Holy Place where the ark of the covenant was kept. He also built a residence for himself called the Palace of the Forest of Lebanon, which showcased the wealth of the Israelite nation. In the tenth chapter of the Old Testament book of 1 Kings, we are given a glimpse of the glory of Solomon's reign.

> Now when the queen of Sheba heard of the fame of Solomon concerning the name of the LORD, she came to test him with hard questions. She came to Jerusalem with a very great retinue, with camels bearing spices and very

much gold and precious stones. And when she came to Solomon, she told him all that was on her mind. And Solomon answered all her questions; there was nothing hidden from the king that he could not explain to her. And when the queen of Sheba had seen all the wisdom of Solomon, the house that he had built, the food of his table, the seating of his officials, and the attendance of his servants, their clothing, his cupbearers, and his burnt offerings that he offered at the house of the LORD, there was no more breath in her. . . .

Now the weight of gold that came to Solomon in one year was 666 talents [50,000 lbs.] of gold, besides that which came from the explorers and from the business of the merchants, and from all the kings of the west and from the governors of the land. King Solomon made 200 large shields of beaten gold; 600 shekels [15 lbs.] of gold went into each shield. And he made 300 shields of beaten gold; three minas of gold [3.75 lbs.] went into each shield. And the king put them in the House of the Forest of Lebanon. The king also made a great ivory throne and overlaid it with the finest gold. The throne had six steps, and the throne had a round top, and on each side of the seat were armrests and two lions standing beside the armrests, while twelve lions stood there, one on each end of a step on the six steps. The like of it was never made in any kingdom. All King Solomon's drinking vessels were of gold, and all the vessels of the House of the Forest of Lebanon were of pure gold. None were of silver; silver was not considered as anything in the days of Solomon. For the king had a fleet of ships of Tarshish at sea with the fleet of Hiram. Once every three years the fleet of ships of Tarshish used to come bringing gold, silver, ivory, apes, and peacocks.

Thus King Solomon excelled all the kings of the earth in riches and in wisdom. And the whole earth sought the presence of Solomon to hear his wisdom, which God had put into his mind. Every one of them brought his present, articles of silver and gold, garments, myrrh, spices, horses, and mules, so much year by year. (1 Kings 10:1–5, 14–24 ESV)

Jerusalem in Solomon's day was an amazingly fabulous city. There was gold everywhere and, oddly enough, even some apes and peacocks. The temple was covered in gold with gold utensils, and there was a wall that ran all around the city to protect it from any besieging army.

As mentioned earlier in this book, the end of Solomon's life was marked by a growing distance from God as he embraced aspects of the foreign religions around him. After his death the kingdom was split in two and over the next 350 years or so both kingdoms followed a path that led them farther and farther from God. In 722 BC the Assyrian kingdom captured the northern kingdom and its capital city of Samaria; the southern kingdom of Judah, with its capital in Jerusalem, was able to hold out. The city still had the temple and was surrounded by a defensive wall. Many of the inhabitants probably thought God would not allow anything to happen to the city where the temple stood. However, successive kings became more and more depraved and some even set up idols and altars to foreign gods in the temple itself. God sent multiple prophets to warn the people about the consequences of their actions to no avail.

Finally, around 605 BC, the Babylonians under King Nebuchadnezzar attacked and defeated the city of Jerusalem. They took many of its inhabitants into exile (likely including Daniel), but left the city largely intact. Although he took most of the remaining treasures that Solomon had acquired and made for the palace and temple, there is no record of the destruction of the city itself. He removed the current king Jehoiachin from the throne and replaced him with his uncle Mattaniah, renamed Zedekiah. After that Nebuchadnezzar returned to his own kingdom, and seems to have left Zedekiah to run the kingdom as a vassal state, likely paying annual tribute to Babylon.

For some reason, after ruling for nine years, Zedekiah decided to roll the dice and rebel against his overlord. Keeping in mind that Babylon was the strongest military in the world at that time, and that Nebuchadnezzar had already taken "all the officers and fighting men" of Judah into exile, it doesn't seem to be a very

well-thought-out decision. Somewhat predictably, Nebuchadnezzar returned to punish the rebellious city and things did not go
well for Zedekiah. If Nebuchadnezzar had been merciful the first
time he conquered Jerusalem, he was determined to make an example of it on this go-round.

> And in the ninth year of his reign, in the tenth month,
> on the tenth day of the month, Nebuchadnezzar king of
> Babylon came with all his army against Jerusalem and
> laid siege to it. And they built siegeworks all around it.
> So the city was besieged till the eleventh year of King
> Zedekiah. On the ninth day of the fourth month the
> famine was so severe in the city that there was no food
> for the people of the land. Then a breach was made in the
> city, and all the men of war fled by night by the way of
> the gate between the two walls, by the king's garden, and
> the Chaldeans [Babylonians] were around the city. And
> they went in the direction of the Arabah. But the army
> of the Chaldeans pursued the king and overtook him in
> the plains of Jericho, and all his army was scattered from
> him. Then they captured the king and brought him up to
> the king of Babylon at Riblah, and they passed sentence
> on him. They slaughtered the sons of Zedekiah before his
> eyes, and put out the eyes of Zedekiah and bound him in
> chains and took him to Babylon. . . .
> And he burned the house of the Lord and the king's
> house and all the houses of Jerusalem; every great house
> he burned down. And all the army of the Chaldeans,
> who were with the captain of the guard, broke down the
> walls around Jerusalem. And the rest of the people who
> were left in the city and the deserters who had deserted
> to the king of Babylon, together with the rest of the mul-
> titude, Nebuzaradan the captain of the guard carried into
> exile. But the captain of the guard left some of the poor-
> est of the land to be vinedressers and plowmen. (2 Kings
> 25:1–7, 9–12 ESV)

In the aftermath, the once proud city of Jerusalem was left a wasteland. The fabulous temple and palace were burned to the ground,
the wall around the city was completely destroyed and the royal

family was slaughtered. Only "some of the poorest of the land" were left to farm in the ruins of the city. This fall from grace—the transformation of Jerusalem from a glorious symbol of Israel's status as God's favored nation to a deserted ghost town—is the backdrop for the story of Nehemiah, which takes place roughly a century after Daniel's escape from the lion's den.

Although a few people had been allowed to return to Jerusalem, most of the Jewish nation was still living in exile under Persian rule. Nehemiah is introduced in the first chapter of the book that bears his name as a Jew serving in the court of the Persian king Artaxerxes. Specifically, Nehemiah served as the cupbearer to the king. Only someone trusted implicitly by the king could serve as cupbearer; the job entailed guarding the king's wine and food closely to make sure that it wasn't poisoned before the king got it. Kings at that time were hypervigilant when it came to the possibility of assassination, and for good reason: Artaxerxes's father, Xerxes, had been assassinated by the captain of his bodyguard. His oldest son, Darius, was next in line for the throne, but *he* was assassinated by Artaxerxes. The Old Testament books of 1 Kings and 2 Kings list no fewer than eleven rulers who fell to assassins. So you can see how history and the course of his own rise to power would have made Artaxerxes leery of the people around him. Consequently, we can assume that Nehemiah was implicitly trusted by the king, guarding his food and likely even tasting his wine before the king would take it.

The story of Nehemiah begins with him serving in this role in the king's palace. He met one of his countrymen, Hanani, who had recently been to Judah, the southern kingdom that contained the city of Jerusalem. Approximately ninety years earlier, around 530 BC, another Persian king (Cyrus, who ruled during the time of Daniel) had allowed a relatively small number of Jews to return there and live in the city of Jerusalem. Nehemiah asked Hanani how things were going with the people who had returned. The report he got was not good: "The remnant there in the province who had survived the exile is in great trouble and shame. The wall of Jerusalem is broken down, and its gates are destroyed by fire" (Neh. 1:3 ESV).

Nehemiah, a devout Jew, was understandably upset to hear of the distress of his people. He was so distraught that he was unable to conceal it from those around him. Artaxerxes cared for Nehemiah enough that he noticed his despair and questioned him about it: "The king said to me, 'Why is your face sad, seeing you are not sick? This is nothing but sadness of the heart'" (Neh. 2:2 ESV).

Many times when someone asks, "How are you doing?," they don't really want to hear about your problems. It's just something to say, and they want to hear you say, "Fine, thanks. How are you?," even if you are currently bleeding out on the floor. Nehemiah either knew the king well enough to know that there was actual interest behind the question or he took a big risk. Instead of pretending that everything was okay, he chose to lay out his troubles to his superior. He must not have been completely sure of himself, though, because the text reveals that he was nervous.

> Then I was very much afraid. I said to the king, "Let the king live forever! Why should not my face be sad, when the city, the place of my fathers' graves, lies in ruins, and its gates have been destroyed by fire?" (Neh. 2:3 ESV).

It is important to keep in mind that the Persian Empire was the largest in the world at that time. There had been at least two major rebellions in the previous ten years (in Egypt and the Trans-Euphrates) that had required immediate and direct attention. Surely there were a myriad of other administrative details that Artaxerxes had to deal with in order to keep things running smoothly, so it would be fair to assume that the plight of a small Jewish town in the backwater of his empire would not be high on his priority list. Nehemiah went for it, though, and when the king asked him what should be done about it Nehemiah became even bolder.

> I said to the king, "If it pleases the king, and if your servant has found favor in your sight, that you send me to Judah, to the city of my fathers' graves, that I may rebuild it." And the king said to me (the queen sitting beside him), "How long will you be gone, and when will you

return?" So it pleased the king to send me when I had given him a time. And I said to the king, "If it pleases the king, let letters be given me to the governors of the province Beyond the River, that they may let me pass through until I come to Judah, and a letter to Asaph, the keeper of the king's forest, that he may give me timber to make beams for the gates of the fortress of the temple, and for the wall of the city, and for the house that I shall occupy." (Neh. 2:5–8a ESV)

Nehemiah basically asked for an extended vacation, leaving the king without his trusted advisor/bodyguard/poison shield for the foreseeable future. In addition, he asked for the king to foot the bill for all the wood needed to rebuild the temple, the wall around the whole city, and Nehemiah's own personal house. That took some guts—or some serious faith. The text tells us that Nehemiah prayed to God before making the request and was quick to credit God for his success: "And the king granted me what I asked, for the good hand of my God was upon me" (Neh. 2:8b ESV).

So, his gamble having paid off, Nehemiah set off for Jerusalem with letters of authorization from the king and an escort of army officers and cavalry to keep him safe. After settling in for a few days, he rode around the length of the wall at night to inspect the damage. The rubble was piled high enough in some places that there wasn't enough room for his horse to get through. After assessing the damage and seeing for himself the extent of work that needed to be done, Nehemiah took his plan to the people living in the ruined city.

> Then I said to them, "You see the trouble we are in, how Jerusalem lies in ruins with its gates burned. Come, let us build the wall of Jerusalem, that we may no longer suffer derision." And I told them of the hand of my God that had been upon me for good, and also of the words that the king had spoken to me. And they said, "Let us rise up and build." So they strengthened their hands for the good work. (Neh. 2:17–18 ESV)

Nehemiah convinced the Israelites living there to work with him. The third chapter of the book of Nehemiah details how he divided the job up among families, having them work on sections of the wall near their respective residences. While it is not super-exciting to read, it is a testament to Nehemiah's dedication and organizational skills. The community came together and the wall slowly started to rise up from the ruins.

Around this point we are introduced to the villains of the story, Sanballat and Tobiah, who were likely the governors of the surrounding areas of Samaria and Ammon. They were in a position to treat the pathetic Jewish remnant however they pleased and were not very excited about the idea of a defensive wall going up around the city. Their response went from concern to mockery to open aggression.

> But when Sanballat the Horonite and Tobiah the Ammonite servant heard this, it displeased them greatly that someone had come to seek the welfare of the people of Israel. (Neh. 2:10 ESV)
>
> But when Sanballat the Horonite and Tobiah the Ammonite servant and Geshem the Arab heard of it, they jeered at us and despised us and said, "What is this thing that you are doing? Are you rebelling against the king?" (Neh. 2:19 ESV)
>
> Now when Sanballat heard that we were building the wall, he was angry and greatly enraged, and he jeered at the Jews. And he said in the presence of his brothers and of the army of Samaria, "What are these feeble Jews doing? Will they restore it for themselves? Will they sacrifice? Will they finish up in a day? Will they revive the stones out of the heaps of rubbish, and burned ones at that?" Tobiah the Ammonite was beside him, and he said, "Yes, what they are building—if a fox goes up on it he will break down their stone wall!" (Neh. 4:1–3 ESV)
>
> But when Sanballat and Tobiah and the Arabs and the Ammonites and the Ashdodites heard that the repairing of the walls of Jerusalem was going forward and that the breaches were beginning to be closed, they were very angry. And they all plotted together to come

and fight against Jerusalem and to cause confusion in it.
(Neh. 4:7–8 ESV)

Nehemiah rallied the workers, who were understandably concerned about the prospect of being attacked. He split them into two groups and had one group work while the other half stood guard with weapons and armor. Nehemiah constantly patrolled the perimeter, traveling with a trumpeter who could quickly summon the armed force to meet any attack. Nehemiah encouraged the people, telling them, "Do not be afraid of them. Remember the Lord, who is great and awesome, and fight for your brothers, your sons, your daughters, your wives, and your homes" (Neh. 4:14 ESV).

As you read through his story, it is hard not to be impressed by Nehemiah's leadership ability. He kept the people organized, enthused, and motivated. He calmed their fears by focusing on the job at hand and reminded them that God was watching over them. As the wall grew nearer and nearer to completion, the dastardly duo of Sanballat and Tobiah continued to do their best to sow confusion. They threatened violence, tried to lure Nehemiah into an assassination attempt, and then tried to halt the work by sending a letter to Artaxerxes saying that Nehemiah had declared himself king in Jerusalem.

In addition to these outside threats, Nehemiah had to deal with turmoil from within his own forces. Many people had worked on the wall instead of working in their fields and now had no crops and no money to buy food. Some landowners had borrowed money from other Jews or mortgaged their fields and vineyards to pay the Persian tax on their land. Now, possibly because of a famine or poor crop yield, they were unable to pay their debts. Some lost their land while others had to subject their children to slavery to pay off what they owed. In many cases these debts were held by fellow Israelites who were unsympathetic to the plight of their countrymen.

This was a critical moment. It was relatively easy to unite the people against a common outside enemy, but there was no way to resolve this issue without potentially losing support from a critical faction of his own people. If he demanded justice and compassion from the wealthy nobles, Nehemiah ran the risk of having them turn on him and possibly siding with his enemies Sanballat and Tobiah. On the other hand, if he turned a blind eye to the injustice he could lose the respect and loyalty of the rank and file who were doing most of the work. In the end, Nehemiah determined to do what was right and trusted God to sort out the details:

> I was very angry when I heard their outcry and these words. I took counsel with myself, and I brought charges against the nobles and the officials. I said to them, "You are exacting interest, each from his brother." And I held a great assembly against them and said to them, "We, as far as we are able, have bought back our Jewish brothers who have been sold to the nations, but you even sell your brothers that they may be sold to us!" They were silent and could not find a word to say. So I said, "The thing that you are doing is not good. Ought you not to walk in the fear of our God to prevent the taunts of the nations our enemies? Moreover, I and my brothers and my servants are lending them money and grain. Let us abandon this exacting of interest. Return to them this very day their fields, their vineyards, their olive orchards, and their houses, and the percentage of money, grain, wine, and oil that you have been exacting from them." Then they said, "We will restore these and require nothing from them. We will do as you say." And I called the priests and made them swear to do as they had promised. (Neh. 5:6–12 ESV)

Nehemiah publicly confronted the nobles with their wrongdoing and convinced them to restore what they had taken in addition to putting a stop to their predatory lending. As a result, the work continued and soon the entire wall was finished.

To commemorate the occasion and dedicate the wall, Nehemiah, along with Ezra the priest, had all the people gather in a square before one of the gates. There the Law was read from a scroll to all the people. It wasn't just a quick review—the reading took *six hours* to finish. Nehemiah, knowing that there likely had not been any significant instruction in the Law for more than seventy years, had trained Levites there to interpret the Law and help the people understand what they were hearing. It must have been a long day, but it served its purpose. The people, upon hearing the Law, became aware of the extent to which they had transgressed it. Nehemiah 8:9 says that "all the people had been weeping as they listened to the words of the Law."

This penitent attitude led to a large assembly where everyone participated in a corporate confession of their sins and pledged to do their best to follow God's law as scrupulously as possible in the future. Finally, Nehemiah finished dedicating the wall in a ceremony involving two choirs singing praises from atop the wall and massive sacrifices to honor God.

The book of Nehemiah ends after detailing two final conflicts. Nehemiah returned to serve Artaxerxes in the capital twelve years after he had begun his quest to repair the wall around Jerusalem. While there he heard that his old enemy, Tobiah, had been granted a room in the new temple as a living space. Nehemiah, angry at this desecration of a space meant for worship, obtained permission to go back to Jerusalem one more time. When he arrived at the temple he promptly threw all of Tobiah's belongings out in the street, purified the room, and returned it to its original use. Nehemiah also learned that foreign traders were bringing their wares into Jerusalem and setting up a market to sell them on the Sabbath, a day that the Law of Moses set aside for rest and not for business. He talked with the merchants and threatened to arrest them if they continued to show up on the Sabbath. For good measure he locked the gates of the city at sunset on the night before the Sabbath and posted hand-picked guards to make sure no one entered until the following day. His zeal for the Lord made Nehemiah an integral part in both the rebuilding of the city and in maintaining the integrity of the temple and the Sabbath.

SO WHAT?

As with the other stories we have looked at, it is worth asking what possible tie there might be between this somewhat obscure historical account and the story of Jesus. What, if anything, can we learn about Jesus as we read the account of Nehemiah and his efforts? *Are* these stories related? As you read through this story the first time, it may be hard to see how it relates to Jesus. However, there are several crucial similarities.

1. *Nehemiah was a cupbearer to the king.* That is, he served in a trusted position at the king's side. When he heard of the desperate plight of his countrymen, he was willing to leave the relative ease of his life in the palace and make the hazardous journey to Jerusalem, a place where he would be in constant danger.

   According to the New Testament, Jesus left a position in heaven at the right hand of God in order to save the people of God from their plight. His life was constantly in danger as he traveled around Jerusalem and the surrounding countryside.

2. *Nehemiah was constantly opposed and threatened by Sanballat and Tobiah.* Likely governors of the area before Nehemiah arrived, Sanballat and Tobiah saw his efforts as a threat to their authority. Tobiah apparently had ties to the Jewish priesthood and he used his connections to try and undermine Nehemiah. These two figures used intimidation, intrigue, and lies to try and thwart Nehemiah in his work.

   Jesus was constantly opposed by the elders and scribes of the Jewish nation. They were the undisputed leaders of Hebrew society before he arrived, but they quickly found their authority and personal righteousness challenged by Jesus's teaching. They also used intimidation, intrigue, and lies in an effort to discredit Jesus and put an end to his work.

3. *Nehemiah helped rebuild the wall around Jerusalem and the temple* (the rebuilding of the temple is recorded in the companion book of Ezra). By doing so he helped provide a

safe place for the people to live and worship, which in turn allowed them to start observing the festivals and commandments decreed in the Law of Moses.

Jesus also came to build a temple and to provide the children of God with a place to worship. In John 2:19 Jesus told the Jewish leaders, "Destroy this temple, and I will raise it again in three days."

The apostle Peter later clarified Jesus's claim to his followers:

> As you come to him, a living stone rejected by men but in the sight of God chosen and precious, you yourselves like living stones are being built up as a spiritual house, to be a holy priesthood, to offer spiritual sacrifices acceptable to God through Jesus Christ. For it stands in Scripture:
> "Behold, I am laying in Zion a stone, a cornerstone chosen and precious, and whoever believes in him will not be put to shame." (1 Peter 2:4–6 ESV)

The last portion is a prophecy from Isaiah 28:16, which shows that the motif of Jesus as the cornerstone of a new temple bridges the Old and New testaments.

4. *Nehemiah was a guardian for the masses of poor and lower class in Jerusalem.* When the nobles were confiscating their land and selling children into indentured servitude to pay off debts, Nehemiah angrily confronted them in a public forum. His intervention led to a cessation of the oppressive practices and brought relief to the oppressed in Jerusalem.

When Jesus saw the state of the people of Israel he had compassion on them. Matthew 9:36 says, "When he saw the crowds, he had compassion for them, because they were harassed and helpless, like sheep without a shepherd." Throughout the New Testament he angrily confronts the scribes, Pharisees, and experts in the Law who functioned as cold, sterile, merciless authority figures instead of showing the love of God to the masses. One such encounter is recorded in Luke 11:46, where Jesus says, "And you experts in the law, woe to you, because you load people down with burdens they can hardly carry, and you yourselves will not lift one finger to help them."

5. *Nehemiah assembled the people for a reading of the Law and had Levites and priests there to explain it to them.* After reading the Law he led the people in a confession of their sins in order to turn their hearts back to God.

Jesus constantly taught the Law to large groups of people. The Sermon on the Mount, recorded in Matthew 5–7, begins with these words: "And seeing the multitudes, he went up into a mountain: and when he was set, his disciples came unto him: And he opened his mouth, and taught them, saying . . ." (Matt. 5:1–2 KJV). Jesus also interpreted the Law for them. He frequently used phrases like, "You have heard that it was said to the people long ago . . . but I tell you . . ." in order to make sure that his listeners could see past the letter of the Law to understand its true intent. He used parables, or stories from everyday life, throughout his entire ministry to help people better understand the kingdom of God.

6. *Nehemiah cleansed the temple from the presence of a secular leader*, and put an end to buying and selling that desecrated the Sabbath day.

Jesus also cleansed the temple of Jewish leaders who were using the Court of the Gentiles to sell animals for sacrifice. He put an end to the selling of merchandise that desecrated the temple area where people were supposed to worship. The event is recorded in John 2:14–17 (ESV):

> In the temple he found those who were selling oxen and sheep and pigeons, and the money-changers sitting there. And making a whip of cords, he drove them all out of the temple, with the sheep and oxen. And he poured out the coins of the money-changers and overturned their tables. And he told those who sold the pigeons, "Take these things away; do not make my Father's house a house of trade." His disciples remembered that it was written, "Zeal for your house will consume me."

Again, you may ask: So what? Are these similarities mere coincidence? Or is the story of Nehemiah coming to the rescue of God's people a foreshadowing of the story of Christ? If so, what lessons are there to be learned about Jesus?

First, Nehemiah's response to Hanani's report on the conditions that the people of Jerusalem were living in reveals his deep love for his brothers and sisters: "As soon as I heard these words I sat down and wept and mourned for days, and I continued fasting and praying before the God of heaven" (Neh. 1:4 ESV). Nehemiah was so grieved by the state of his people that he wept and mourned *for days*. His distress was such that when he interacted with Artaxerxes, the king immediately detected his deep sorrow. It was deep enough that Nehemiah was willing to leave a safe, stable, comfortable life in the palace and go to a place so dangerous that he would spend much of the next year sleeping with a sword and spear.

The message of the Bible is that Jesus loves each of us, including you, deeply enough to make the same sacrifice. Philippians 2:5–8 (ESV) tells us, "Have this mind among yourselves, which is yours in Christ Jesus, who, though he was in the form of God, did not count equality with God a thing to be grasped, but emptied himself, by taking the form of a servant, being born in the likeness of men. And being found in human form, he humbled himself by becoming obedient to the point of death, even death on a cross."

The New Testament reveals in Jesus a sorrow in our separation from God every bit as profound as Nehemiah's distress upon hearing of the state of the refugees in Jerusalem.

> When Jesus saw her weeping, and the Jews who had come with her also weeping, he was deeply moved in his spirit and greatly troubled. And he said, "Where have you laid him?" They said to him, "Lord, come and see." Jesus wept. So the Jews said, "See how he loved him!" (John 11:33–36 ESV)

> O Jerusalem, Jerusalem, the city that kills the prophets and stones those who are sent to it! How often would I have gathered your children together as a hen gathers her

brood under her wings, and you were not willing! (Luke
13:34 ESV)

The New Testament is filled with verses like the ones above that
show the deep love Christ had for the people he ministered to.
Like Nehemiah, Jesus's love and compassion for God's distressed
children compelled him to leave the safety of the kingdom and
enter a world where he was harassed and constantly in danger.

Secondly, just as Nehemiah, with God's help, was able to
achieve his goal of building a wall to protect the Israelites from
the threats in the world around them, Jesus also accomplished his
mission. The fact that Jesus came to build something similar is
evident in the imagery of construction found throughout the New
Testament.

> Everyone who hears these words of mine and puts them
> into practice is like a wise man who built his house on
> the rock. The rain came down, the streams rose, and the
> winds blew and beat against that house; yet it did not
> fall, because it had its foundation on the rock. (Matt.
> 7:24–25)

> He said to them, "But who do you say that I am?" Simon
> Peter replied, "You are the Christ, the Son of the living
> God." And Jesus answered him, "Blessed are you, Simon
> Bar-Jonah! For flesh and blood has not revealed this to
> you, but my Father who is in heaven. And I tell you, you
> are Peter, and on this rock I will build my church, and the
> gates of hell shall not prevail against it." (Matt. 16:15–18
> ESV)

Furthermore, the writer of the New Testament book of Hebrews
tells us how Jesus has brought us to a new Jerusalem:

> But you have come to Mount Zion, to the city of the
> living God, the heavenly Jerusalem. You have come to
> thousands upon thousands of angels in joyful assembly,
> to the church of the firstborn, whose names are written
> in heaven. You have come to God, the Judge of all, to
> the spirits of the righteous made perfect, to Jesus the
> mediator of a new covenant, and to the sprinkled blood

that speaks a better word than the blood of Abel. (Heb. 12:22–24)

Through his death and resurrection Jesus built a new spiritual temple that provides atonement for all who believe. Just as the wall around Jerusalem protected the ancient Israelites from those who wished to do them harm, Christ provides a safe haven for all who believe.

IS THAT ALL?

We have finally reached the end of our narrative. It would be nice to say that the Israelites lived happily ever after, but sadly that was not to be. They came under the dominion of Alexander the Great around 333 BC and, with the exception of one short period of self-rule, would live subject to other nations until the Roman Empire, responding to a Jewish rebellion, overran Jerusalem and destroyed the temple in 70 AD. Did the destruction of the temple (again) signal the end of the Jewish nation and the Jewish faith?

Many other people groups that lived alongside the Israelites in Old Testament times (the Hittites, Amorites, Philistines and others) vanished from the pages of history. The Jewish nation, and the Old Testament stories that document their origin, have endured. Is that a result of luck, random chance, or divine intervention? The answer to that question is largely determined by whether or not the Old Testament has any significant relevance for us today. Let's take one last, quick look back at what we've read—and take a final, closer look at one story from the very beginning of this book.

Conclusion

Abraham, Sacrifice, and the Conclusion of the Conclusion

Our story began in Genesis with God making a promise to Abraham, swearing that Abraham would become the father of a great nation and that all peoples would be blessed through him. The five stories that followed showed how God revealed details about how Abraham's descendant, Jesus, would become that promised blessing. As we close out this study, I would like to take a moment to examine the story of Abraham and see one final way in which God dramatically foretold exactly how Jesus would save all nations as promised.

The story of Abraham begins in Genesis 12, following a long, somewhat tedious genealogy in the second half of the previous chapter. A genealogy is just a listing of the names of successive members of a family; this one starts with Noah's son Shem, and ends with a man named Terah. Terah had three sons, one of whom was Abram (who would later become Abraham). We are given three important facts about Abram. First, he lived in the land of the Chaldeans, or Babylonians. Second, he was married to a woman named Sarai. Third, and perhaps most relevant to our story, Sarai was barren, meaning that she had not had any children. At this time Abraham was seventy-five years old. Sarai was ten years younger, which meant that at sixty-five, her odds of ever having children would have seemed nonexistent.

The story begins in chapter 12 of Genesis, with the first of three major events in Abraham's life.

> The LORD had said to Abram, "Go from your country, your people and your father's household to the land I will show you. I will make you into a great nation, and I will bless you; I will make your name great, and you will be a blessing. I will bless those who bless you, and whoever curses you I will curse; and all peoples on earth will be blessed through you." So Abram went, as the LORD had told him. (Gen. 12:1–4)

Initially Abram is not distinguished from any other people in the genealogy; there is no verse that says, "And Terah gave birth to Abram, who was one righteous dude." Without explaining whether or not God chose Abram randomly or because of some aspect of his character, Abram becomes the focus of the story as God speaks to him.

There are a few interesting things to note. Again, there is no indication that Abram had any prior knowledge or relationship with God. The Chaldean civilization believed in a pantheon of gods similar to those in Greek mythology, with names like Enlil, Nintur and Enki. These gods were frequently at odds with each other and only created people to do the tedious work that the deities were tired of doing. Each city had its own patron god and maintained one temple for the deity and a smaller temple for his spouse. Each temple had an idol to represent its divine sponsor and a staff that would prepare food for and sometimes even bathe and dress the idol. Prayers and petitions could be made of the god if they were accompanied by a sacrifice. The religion was based on the idea that if the people adequately supplied the needs of whichever god ruled their city, they might get favors dispensed in return.

There are no details given about how God first spoke to Abram. Later in the story he communicates with Abram through visions, so perhaps this was done the same way. Did Abram hear a disembodied voice, or see a physical manifestation of God? We don't know, but whatever it was must have been pretty convincing. God wasn't asking Abram to run down to the corner for a loaf of bread; he told him to leave his country, his people, and his father's house—essentially, to abandon everything he knew, everything familiar in his life. To go where? "To the land I will show you." What? Get up and leave everything I have and everyone I know to go someplace that you'll tell me about *after* I'm on my way?

However God communicated with Abram, it was effective. I feel like that if the local priest had told Abram, "Oh yeah, Enki says you're supposed to move out into the middle of nowhere all by yourself," things might not have turned out the same way. Fortunately for Abram, God coupled his challenging command with an equally huge promise: namely, that Abram would become a great nation and that, eventually, *all peoples* on earth would be blessed through him.

So however it happened, God's message convinced the progenitor of the Hebrew nation to pack up his possessions and with his wife move to the land of Canaan, a place that he knew nothing about. His life there was not dull; the next few chapters of Genesis tell how he and Sarai had to flee to Egypt in the midst of a famine, and how he led a band of followers against a coalition of four marauding kings in a raid to rescue his cousin Lot. All this time he waited for God to fulfill his promise. Years later the Lord appeared to him again to reiterate his commitment to Abram, and finally the faithful servant asked the question that must have been worrying him. "Sovereign LORD, what can you give me since I remain childless . . . ? You have given me no children; so a servant in my house will be my heir" (Gen. 15:2–3).

God replied, "a son who is your own flesh and blood will be your heir. . . . Look up at the heavens and count the stars, if indeed you can count them. So shall your offspring be" (Genesis 15:4–5). Keeping in mind that Abram was likely in his eighties at this point and his wife Sarai was only ten years younger, it must have seemed pretty unbelievable that they were ever going to raise kids of their own. Nonetheless, we are told that "Abram believed the Lord, and he credited it to him as righteousness." (Gen. 15:6).

So Abram and Sarai endured, waiting for the promise of the Lord to come true. Finally, though, around the time Abram turned eighty-five, they decided to take things into their own hands. "Now Sarai, Abram's wife, had borne him no children. But she had an Egyptian maidservant named Hagar, so she said to Abram, 'The Lord has kept me from having children. Go, sleep with my maidservant; perhaps I can build a family through her.' Abram agreed with what Sarai said. . . . He slept with Hagar, and she conceived" (Genesis 16:1–2, 4).

To modern readers many aspects of this part of the story are troubling. An older wife telling her husband to sleep with a much younger girl just to get her pregnant is pretty creepy. And Hagar, as a slave, is given no choice in the matter. I mean, it's possible she could have been attracted to Abram and happy to sleep with him, but it is probably more likely that she had to play her part whether she wanted to or not. If this part of the story makes you angry or disgusted, it is important to remember that this is not how God intended for things to play out. This sequence of events was the result of Abram and Sarai trying to do things their own way, and it would have major consequences for the entire family going forward.

So, from a sad beginning a boy named Ishmael was born to Hagar and raised in Abram's house. Not surprisingly, Hagar and Sarai did not get along too well. At one point things got so bad that Hagar fled with her young son in tow. Wandering in the desert, she was told by a messenger of the Lord to return to her mistress, and so Ishmael continued to be raised by Abram, who likely considered him to be the promised heir.

Things continued that way for thirteen years. Ishmael grew into a teenager, Abram assumed that he had been given his heir, and Sarai likely assumed that she was a footnote in the story, doomed to obscurity by her inability to have children. There is no indication that Abram had any communication from God during all those long years and he may have assumed that there would be no more visions or messages. Then, when Abram was ninety-nine years old, everything changed.

There are two meetings detailed between Abram and God in the seventeenth and eighteenth chapters of Genesis. In the first meeting God appeared to reaffirm his covenant with Abram, stating again that he would make Abram the father of many nations and that one day his descendants would occupy the land of Canaan. This time, though, God added a surprising proviso: "As for Sarai your wife, you are no longer to call her Sarai; her name will be Sarah. I will bless her and will surely give you a son by her. I will bless her so that she will be the mother of nations; kings of peoples will come from her" (Gen. 17:15–16).

Abram, whose name God had also now changed to Abraham, was not sure he understood. "Abraham fell facedown: he laughed and said to himself, 'Will a son be born to a man a hundred years old? Will Sarah bear a child at the age of ninety?' And Abraham said to God, 'If only Ishmael might live under your blessing!'" (Gen. 17:17–18).

God confirmed that his promise to Abraham would be fulfilled through a son born to Sarah, although Ishmael too would become a great nation. Soon after, Abraham and Sarah were visited by the Lord in the form of three visitors. Abraham offered to give the three travelers food and drink when they passed by his tent. They agreed to stay and as they ate the Lord told Abraham "I will surely return to you about this time next year, and Sarah your wife will have a son" (Gen. 18:10).

Sarah, listening at the entrance to the tent, overheard the prediction but laughed at the thought of giving birth at ninety years old. However, just as God promised, Sarah became pregnant and gave birth to a baby boy. They named him Isaac, which means "he laughs." Sarah said that God had brought her laughter and that everyone who heard would laugh with her. Isaac grew up in a house with very old parents who undoubtedly loved him as much as any child ever had been. To this point, it seems like a pretty happy story. Abraham and Sarah trusted God, waited patiently for years in a foreign land, and were eventually rewarded with their promised child.

To be sure, there were darker aspects to the tale. Hagar was forced into motherhood and mistreated badly enough that she ran away. Sadly, her life did not improve after Isaac was born. Sarah saw Ishmael mocking Isaac and demanded that he be sent away. Abraham did not want to go along with the plan, but after God reassured him that Ishmael would prosper he acquiesced and kicked them out. So, their lives were not all sunshine and roses, but as they raised Isaac they probably felt that they were living a blessed life as a result of their faith.

However, all that came to a screeching halt in one of the most disturbing narratives in the entire Bible. Sometime later, God appeared again to Abraham and told him, "Take your son, your only son, whom you love—Isaac—and go to the region of Moriah. Sacrifice him there as a burnt offering on a mountain I will show you." (Gen. 22:2). No preamble, no explanation, just an abrupt command to go and destroy the one thing in Abraham and Sarah's life that they cared the most about.

In addition to being a living, breathing human being, Isaac was the physical representation of God's faithfulness in keeping his miraculous promises to Abraham. How could any father comply with such a cruel, senseless command to kill his child? I have four children and I love them more than anything in this world. It makes me sick to my stomach to think of any harm coming to them, much less causing them any harm myself. How would Abraham respond?

Some commentators have suggested that because child sacrifice in the ancient world was a common way to show devotion to a god, Abraham may not have seen it as a moral problem. I think that the inclusion of the phrase "your son, your only son, Isaac, whom you love" in the command proves that Isaac was not just some token to be used to display piety but rather the center of his parents' universe. So what would Abraham do? After giving up his family and home to follow God's commands, would he be willing to give up his son? And not just give him up, but to put his son on an altar and kill him in a sacrificial rite? Just reading about it is enough to make any parent queasy, and it is hard to imagine that Abraham did not have the same gut-level reaction.

However, the text reveals that early the next morning he left with Isaac, two servants, and a donkey. He traveled to the mountain that God indicated, left his servants with the donkey, and took Isaac up to build an altar. He then bound Isaac, placed him on the altar, and prepared to sacrifice his son. God intervened at the last minute, saying, "I swear by myself, that because you have not withheld your son, your only son, I will surely bless you and make your descendants as numerous as the stars in the sky and as the sand on the seashore" (Gen. 22:16–17).

Abraham freed Isaac and took him home, where he went on to prosper and have a grandson named Joseph, who would save his family and the fledgling Jewish nation from famine.

What are we to do with this awful story? Do you want to serve a God who ordered a man to kill his son and then, after putting him through that psychological torture, says, "Just kidding! I only wanted to see if you would really do it!" Sarah may not have been able to come to terms with it; as Dennis Prager notes in his commentary on Genesis, Sarah is never mentioned as being with Abraham after the story of Isaac's near-sacrifice.[1] When Sarah's death is recorded later in Genesis, the text indicates that Abraham traveled to where she passed away, which would mean they were not living together at the time. If so, Sarah may not have been able to understand how God could ask Abraham to sacrifice their son or how her husband could have complied. Can you? Can I? How can we resolve this narrative with the idea of a loving, compassionate Creator?

There are at least three ways to view this story. First, God could be a cruel, capricious entity who ordered Abraham to kill his son just to see if he would do it. Like a kid pulling the wings off of a butterfly, a God like that would be curious to see what happened without having any compassion or concern for the participants. In this instance, God would be like a sociopath, curious about people's behavior but totally detached from any concept of or care for their well-being. Or, this story could be about a God who either demanded a test of loyalty or wanted to teach Abraham to trust him no matter what. This is the narrative that I was taught

1. Prager, D. (2019). *The Rational Bible: Genesis* (pp. 263-264). Regnery Faith.

in Sunday school growing up—that Abraham proved his faith by not withholding his most treasured possession and was duly rewarded. Perhaps that is the intended message. In this instance you can appreciate that God was working for Abraham's good in the long-term sense by strengthening his faith, but it is still difficult to understand how God could willingly put a family through the agony of thinking that they were going to have to sacrifice their son.

There is a third possibility, if you are willing to entertain the idea that the Old and New Testament are intended to complement each other.

First, consider the alternative. If you look at the Old Testament as a complete unit by itself, it is hard to see how God completely fulfilled his promise to Abraham. Yes, he was made into a great nation—the Jewish nation that descended from him numbers in the tens or hundreds of millions. Yes, his descendants did occupy Canaan and rule over it; Saul, David, Solomon and others led a kingdom that, at its height, dominated that part of the world. That is all fine and good. But at the end of the Old Testament, there is no way to say that all nations had been blessed through Abraham. So, was the promise ever kept? Was it made by a God who either couldn't or didn't care to follow through on his vow, or is it just an empty tale, another made-up religious myth that people tell?

Now, consider once more the possibility that the Old Testament, written in antiquity, was never intended to stand on its own, but instead was a prelude to the story of Jesus in the New Testament. In this scenario, God *wants* your stomach to turn as you think about Abraham being ordered to sacrifice his son. He wants you to imagine the grief of Abraham and Sarah as they think of voluntarily sacrificing their son, their only son, who they love. As you sit and wonder how anyone could ask Abraham to do such an awful thing, God wants you to hear the words of John 3:16 (ESV, emphasis added): "For God so loved the world, that he gave *his* only Son."

If you subscribe to this viewpoint, then in the Old Testament God is saying: *this* is how I am going to use Abraham's descendant,

Jesus, to bless the entire world. This awful, terrible thing that you don't even want to read about, that Abraham pondered but didn't have to do, *this* is what *I* am going to do to show you how much I love you. Like Joseph, Abraham had many sons but only one beloved son. So too, God calls us all his children but only had one precious, beloved son that he was willing to give up in order to save us all.

CONCLUSION OF THE CONCLUSION

Well, we are finally at the end. Hopefully you now have at least a rough idea of the narrative arc of the Old Testament. God made a promise to Abraham, which was passed down to each of the patriarchs: Isaac, and then Jacob. Jacob's son Joseph led the forefathers of the Jewish nation into Egypt. Initially a safe haven, it became a place where the Israelite nation was hopelessly enslaved for hundreds of years. God claimed Israel as his own people by defeating their oppressors, leading them out of Egypt, and making a lasting covenant with them at Mount Sinai. Moses and Joshua, acting as God's agents, led the people through the wilderness and eventually to the Promised Land of Canaan. There God established them as a kingdom that would eventually become the most powerful force in the region. Unfortunately, the lack of faith that plagued the people from the start of their journey took root in Canaan and eventually became their defining characteristic. After rejecting God as a nation they were overrun, conquered, and exiled from their home. Thankfully, God's love was deep enough that instead of rejecting them completely, he put into play a process that would lead to their salvation.

There is no question that these accounts were written at least hundreds of years before Jesus was born. It is also clear that there are very real similarities between many of the Old Testament characters and Jesus himself. Joseph, a favored son sent to his brothers, betrayed to death by them but eventually rising to a position of power which he used to welcome those same brothers into a land of plenty. The Passover lamb, the blood of which saved God's people from otherwise certain death and delivered them from a land of slavery. Joshua, who helped lead the people of God through the wilderness, who crossed over the river of doubt and fear, returning to offer everyone who would trust in his words an opportunity to live in the Promised Land. Daniel, a righteous man exiled from the Beautiful Land because of the sins of the people, convicted of transgressing a religious law by a foreign power and abandoned to death in the lions' den—then miraculously returned alive and rose to continue serving God. Nehemiah, willing to leave a life of luxury because of the grief he felt for the plight of God's people, who helped rebuild the walls and temple of Jerusalem, taught the people how to truly follow God's law, and cleared the temple of those who were desecrating it.

Now it is up to you to decide. Did God keep his promise to Abraham? Are these Old Testament accounts pictures that point to the ministry and sacrifice of Jesus? If you believe, like me, that the stories we have examined are linked together with that of Jesus then it is not just possible but plain to see that the promise has been kept. That promise means that the resurrection isn't a story that was made up out of desperation but instead represents the fulfillment of God's promised covenant.

Maybe you aren't buying it. Maybe you think the Old Testament is just a bunch of made-up stories written down thousands of years ago that have somehow managed to capture the imagination of knuckleheads like me, who are convinced that they have a deeper meaning. If so, try a simple experiment. First, go back and look at the similarities between the lives of the characters we discussed and the life of Jesus. Now pick three or four other historical figures whom you are familiar with—Alexander the Great, Julius Caesar, Socrates, Joan of Arc, or anyone else you can think of. Take the details of their life stories and try to make as many connections between them and Jesus as you can. How easy is it? If you can convincingly link any story to that of Jesus, then I have wasted your time. However, if you find that these Old Testament stories, written by people with no knowledge of Jesus, are much more similar than any others you can find, maybe they are worth a deeper study.

Is it believable that the details of God's ultimate plan for each of us are hidden in these stories of deliverance? I believe that the similarities between the accounts we looked at and the story of Jesus in the New Testament are too many and too significant to be mere coincidence. You may or may not agree, but I would challenge you to read these Old Testament stories carefully. You can download a free digital copy of the Bible; I have listed the location of each story at the beginning of their respective chapters. If you truly want to make an informed decision about the connection between these stories and the life of Jesus, you will need to do a little more research. Read the eyewitness gospel accounts of Jesus's life in the New Testament—Matthew, Mark, Luke, and John. I know that reading the Bible sounds intimidating, but the gospel accounts themselves are not actually that long. Reading 10–15 minutes daily should enable you to finish each gospel in two weeks or so.

If you, like me, are convinced that the story of Jesus is foretold in the narrative accounts of the Old Testament, then you are left with proof of a force outside of time and the normal laws of nature, a force that bound these histories together over centuries. Discovering the identity of that force and the love he has for you will change your life forever.

.

.